Electric Guitar for Left-Handed Adults

Book 1 - with Video Play-Along Method for Easy Learning Success

Andy Schneider

See streaming video access instructions on the last page of this book

Play Along with this Book!

Stream the free video examples of these exercises

Scan and go now

SEEINGMUSICBOOKS.COM

SEEING MUSIC METHOD BOOKS

©2024 ANDY SCHNEIDER
WWW.SEEINGMUSICBOOKS.COM

Contents

Foundations of Guitar Playing: Posture, Tuning and Strumming — 7
- **Read This First: Start With Great Posture** — 7
- **Time for a Tune-up: All About Tuning** — 8
  - *Standard Tuning* — 8
  - *Non-Standard Tuning* — 8
  - *Electronic Tuners* — 9
  - *Tuning Apps for Devices* — 9
  - *Tuning by Ear* — 9
  - *Tuning Forks & Pitch Pipes* — 10
  - *Tips for Successful Tuning* — 10
  - *Not All Guitars Tune the Same Way* — 10
- **About Guitar Strings** — 10
- **Strumming: Picks vs. Fingers** — 11
- **Electric Guitar Diagram** — 12

How to Read Chord Diagrams: A Beginner's Guide — 13
- **Chord Diagram Basics** — 13
- **How to Read Chord Diagrams** — 14
- **Practical Tips for Reading Chord Diagrams** — 15
- **Learning Bonus - Memorize Your Strings** — 16
- **About Chord Names and Symbols** — 17

Start at Square One: Play Single Notes Cleanly — 19
- **Play Just One Note** — 19
- **Fretting with Precision** — 20
- **Perfect Your Tone** — 21
- **Stopping Your Strings** — 21
- **Understanding Staff Notation** — 22
  - *FAQ: Understanding Note Types and Rhythms* — 22
  - *Reading and Playing Measures* — 24
  - *Subdividing Beats* — 24
- **Single-Note Exercises** — 25

Mastering Your First Chords: G Major and C Major — 27
- **How to Play G Major** — 27
- **G Major - Easy Version** — 28
- **How to Play C Major** — 29
- **C Major - Easy Version** — 30
- **Troubleshoot Your Fretting Hand** — 30
- **Exercises for G and C Chords** — 31

Essential Knowledge: D Major — 33
- **How to Play D Major Using 3 Fingers** — 33
- **D Major - Barre Version** — 34
- **D Major - Easy Version** — 35
- **Exercises for D Major** — 36

Basic Strumming — 37
- **Strumming Basics: Just Down and Up** — 37
- **Strumming Workshop: G Major** — 38
- **Strumming Workshop: E Major** — 39

Setting Up Amps and Effects — 41
- **Introduction to Amplifiers** — 41
  - *Setting Amp Gain and Distortion* — 42
  - *Tailor Your Amp's EQ* — 42
  - *Using Effects* — 43
  - *Standard Pedal Chain Order* — 43
  - *Compressors* — 44
  - *Distortion, Overdrive and Fuzz* — 44
  - *Modulation* — 44
  - *Wah-Wah Pedals* — 45
  - *Reverbs and Delays* — 45
- **Practice Routines with Different Sounds** — 46
  - *Clean Tone Practice* — 46
  - *Distorted Tone Practice* — 46

Big Open Chords: E Major and A Major — 47
- **How to Play E Major** — 47
- **E Major - Easy Version** — 48
- **How to Play A Major** — 49
- **A Major - Easy Version** — 50
- **Rhythmic Exercises** — 50

Learn Minor Chords: E and A Minor — 53
- **How to Play E Minor** — 53
- **E Minor - Easy Version** — 54
- **How to Play A Minor** — 54
- **A Minor - Easy Version** — 55
- **Exercises for A Minor and E Minor** — 56

Rhythm Guitar Gold - Power Chords, Octaves and Chord Fragments — 59
- **Introduction to Power Chords** — 59
  - *What is a Power Chord?* — 59

Play Your First Power Chord — 59
The Basic Shape — 59
Why Play Power Chords? — 60
Clarity in Distortion — 60
Moving Power Chords Up and Down the Neck — 60
Moving Power Chords Across the Neck — 61
Be a Power Chord Powerhouse — 62
Palm Muting and Slides — 62
Tips for Clean Power Chords — 62
Practice Makes Power — 62
E5 and A5 — 62
Octaves — 63
Play Some Octaves — 63
Rhythm Chords — 64
Chop It Up — 64
Arpeggios — 65

Song Workshop: Learn with Your Favorite Styles — 67
Forever Classics — 67
Auld Lang Syne — 67
Swing Low, Sweet Chariot — 68
50's Rock and Roll — 69
Rock, Roll and Rumble — 69
80's Radio — 70
Valley Life Dolls — 70
Midnight Mirage — 71
Old-Time Country & Americana — 72
Whiskey, Wagons, Wheels — 72
A Cowboy on One Knee — 73

Chord and Note Reference — 75

Electric Guitar for Left-Handed Adults

Note to the reader: Figure numbers in this book are from the combination book, Electric Guitar for Left-Handed Adults: Books 1 and 2. Chapters and their figures here are a selection from that combination book.

Learn every note.
Fast and Easy.

Learn it EASY
Learn it FAST
Make it LAST!
With lots of memory-building exercises

SEEING MUSIC METHOD BOOKS

Memorize and Begin Using the Entire Fretboard Quickly and Easily

LEFT-HANDED GUITAR FRETBOARD MEMORIZATION
ANDY SCHNEIDER

BEGINNER TO INTERMEDIATE

Scan to learn more

See more music.
SeeingMusicBooks.com

SEEING MUSIC METHOD BOOKS

Foundations of Guitar Playing: Posture, Tuning and Strumming

GREAT GUITAR PLAYING BEGINS WITH GREAT POSTURE AND INSTRUMENT POSITIONING. YOU'LL FIND IT MUCH EASIER TO REACH THOSE CHORD FINGERINGS.

READ THIS FIRST: START WITH GREAT POSTURE

Fig.1 - Proper Guitar Position

It may seem trivial, but great guitar playing requires good posture. After you align your body and arms, you'll find playing much easier.

Grab the right chair: You'll need to select a chair that keeps your thighs parallel to the ground. Hold your guitar close, allowing the neck to angle slightly upward. This positioning aids in keeping your right hand roughly aligned with your left elbow. If the neck droops, the right hand's reach increases, making playing both challenging and awkward. It's tempting to just flop on the couch with your instrument, but it's really hard to play well that way!

Start with your feet: Elevate your left heel a tiny bit, raising the guitar by about an inch. Observe the position of your right thumb—it should be directly behind the guitar's neck. Coupled with a straight wrist, this alignment is a great start towards good guitar technique. Though maintaining a straight wrist might pose initial challenges, its importance will unveil itself in the subsequent lessons.

Tune and Re-tune: Continually revisit this chapter and reorient your posture as needed. Perfecting basics now speeds up your journey to expertise later.

Fig.2 - Good Hand Position

TIME FOR A TUNE-UP: ALL ABOUT TUNING

Tuning is the first step to ensuring your guitar sounds as it should, offering rich and harmonious tones. Playing on an out-of-tune guitar is no fun. Here's a little background about the often overlooked subject of tuning.

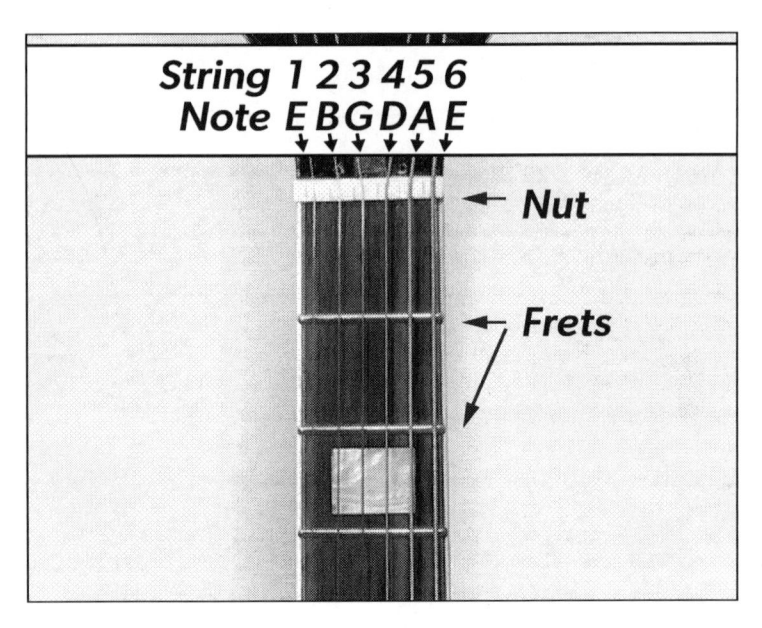

FIG.3 - STANDARD GUITAR TUNING

Common Guitar Tunings - low to high

Standard	E A D G B E
E-flat Standard	E♭ A♭ D♭ G♭ B♭ E♭
DADGAD	D A D G A D
Drop D	D A D G B E
Open G	D G D G B D

FIG.4 - COMMON GUITAR TUNING STYLES

Standard Tuning

You may have heard that some guitarists tune their guitars a little differently than usual. Indeed, there are many different ways to tune the same instrument to acheive different results. Let's look at some of them.

Standard Guitar Tuning: This book uses **Standard Tuning**, which starting from the thickest string (far from the ground) to the thinnest string (closest to the ground), is: E, A, D, G, B, and E.

Non-Standard Tuning

Yes, if there is a Standard Tuning, there must be a non-Standard, too! In fact, there are many, many different ways to tune the guitar. While 99% of guitar music is performed in Standard Tuning, non-standard varieties offer a different sound and opportunities for some creative chords. It should be noted that when playing in non-standard tunings, all of the chords require different fingerings. For this reason, it's best to learn guitar using Standard Tuning, and leave the advanced stuff for a bit later.

Dear DAD: One of the most common non-standard tunings is **DADGAD**, which as you might guess, tunes the guitar D, A, D, G, A, D. This tuning is favorited by blues guitarists and those wishing to play with a slide.

Drop it! Another interesting tuning is **Drop-D**, which is (lowest to highest) D, A, D, G, B and E. Notice how it's identical to Standard tuning, except for the lowest string lowered from E, down one whole-step to D. It's a big rock favorite.

Eb Standard: This is a fun one, favorited by Classic Rock bands like Guns and Roses and Jimi Hendrix. It's a modified version of Standard Tuning where every string is lowered

1/2 step. It goes, E-flat, A-flat, D-flat, G-flat, B-flat, E-flat. Since all the strings are less tight than in Standard, it has a more relaxed feel and a bit darker tone.

Electronic Tuners

Device Type: These are standalone devices, usually pocket-sized, designed exclusively for tuning acoustic or electric stringed instruments.

How to Use: Simply turn it on and, if a clip-on type, clip it to your guitar's headstock. If the unit offers a standard guitar jack and your guitar has a pickup, plug them together so the pickup is sent to the tuner. Pluck a string, and the tuner will display the note you're closest to and whether you're flat (too low), sharp (too high), or in tune.

Advantage: They often come with built-in microphones and the clip-on type can be used in noisy environments, thanks to the clothespin-type attachment feature which detects vibrations directly from the guitar.

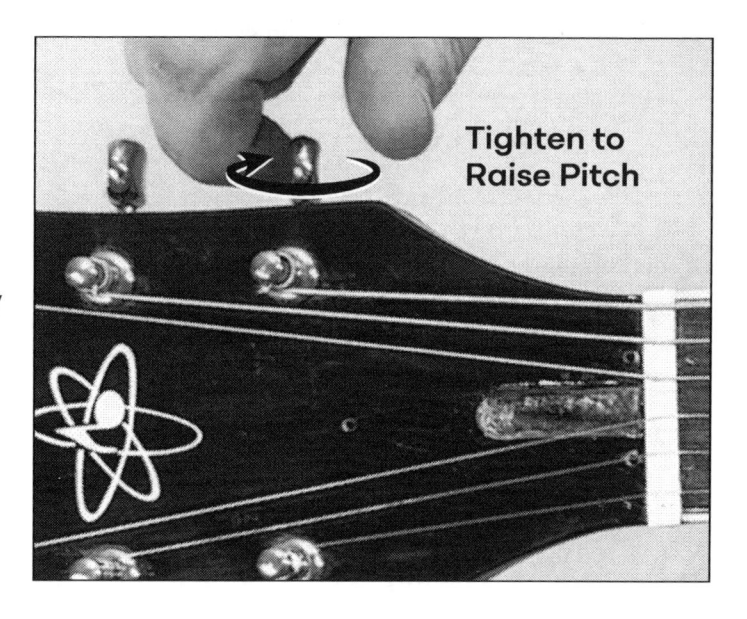

FIG.5 - RAISING PITCH (ON MOST GUITARS)

Tuning Apps for Devices

Device Compatibility: Many modern tuning apps are available for smartphones and tablets.

How to Use: After downloading and opening the app, you'll typically pluck a string, and the app will use your device's microphone to listen and guide you to the correct pitch. Have a look through your phone or device's app store. The free versions are often sufficient for standard tuning, while the premium versions may offer alternate tunings, chord libraries, and more.

Advantage: The convenience of always having a tuner on your phone. Many apps also come with additional features like metronomes or chord libraries.

FIG.6 - USING A CLIP-ON ELECTRONIC TUNER

Tuning by Ear

For seasoned players or those training their ears, you can tune the guitar to itself or another instrument like a piano. Start with one string in tune (often the A or E string), and adjust the other strings relative to that. While this method can be tricky for beginners, it's a valuable skill for any musician.

FOUNDATIONS OF GUITAR PLAYING

Tuning Forks & Pitch Pipes

These are traditional methods. A tuning fork, when struck, resonates at a specific pitch (often A=440 Hz), which you can then use as a reference. Pitch pipes are little, harmonica-like gadgets for tuning reference. When blown into, they produce the note you need to match.

Tips for Successful Tuning

Always Tune UP to a Note: If you go past the desired pitch, lower the string's pitch and then tune up to the correct note. This ensures the string's tension is even and stays in tune longer.

Stretching It: - New strings stretch and may go out of tune more frequently at first. Regular tuning and playing can help them stabilize faster.

Whether you're tuning by ear, using a device, or an app, regularly checking and adjusting your guitar's tuning is crucial. Over time, you'll become faster and more accurate, ensuring your guitar always sounds its best.

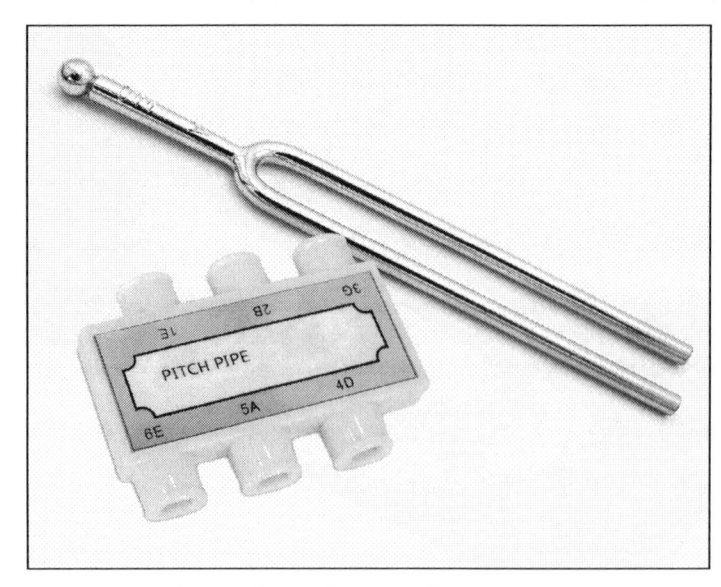

Fig.7 - Pitch Pipe and Tuning Fork

Tuning by Ear?

As your perception of pitch develops, your ears will become great detectors of pitch. This takes a little while, but is a skill worth developing.

Not All Guitars Tune the Same Way

A Word of Caution: Not all guitars have tuning machines that tighten in the same direction. There have been a few that work backwards. On those guitars, turning the keys counter-clockwise doesn't loosen the string, but actually tightens it.

Either way, it's a good idea to always pick the string and listen as you start to turn the key. Make sure the pitch is going the correct direction, up or down.

ABOUT GUITAR STRINGS

The guitar strings are labeled based on their pitch and thickness: the thinnest, highest-pitched string is the first, while the thickest, lowest-pitched one is the sixth.

The Evolution of Guitar Strings

Ancient guitar strings were made from the intestines of sheep, known as *catgut*. Despite the name, no kitties were harmed:)

Fig. 8 - Strumming with a Finger

Guitar body size and shape both help scupt the instrument's tone.

STRUMMING: PICKS VS. FINGERS

Depending on your guitar type, strumming varies. Using a pick provides precision and allows for varied techniques. Hold the pick between your thumb and index finger, ensuring a small portion protrudes. Strumming downwards or upwards produces distinct sounds; practice both.

For classical guitars, which are characterized by their nylon strings, finger-strumming is more traditional. Your thumb, index, middle, and ring fingers each play a role. Alternatively, classical guitarists sometimes use very light picks for certain tones. The goal is to maintain fluidity and precision. As you advance, your fingers or the pick become an extension of your musical expression, allowing you to create melodies that resonate.

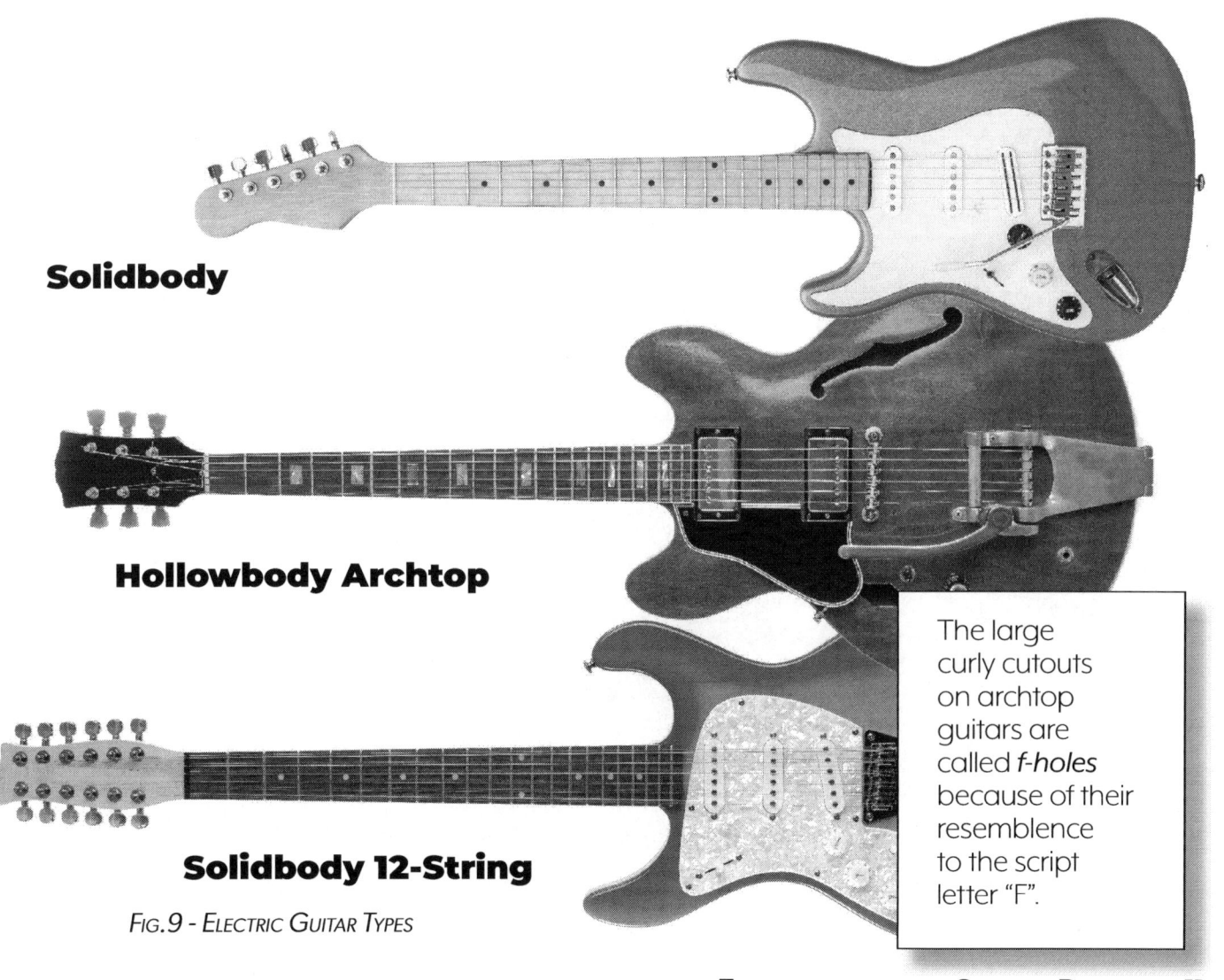

Solidbody

Hollowbody Archtop

Solidbody 12-String

Fig. 9 - Electric Guitar Types

The large curly cutouts on archtop guitars are called *f-holes* because of their resemblence to the script letter "F".

FOUNDATIONS OF GUITAR PLAYING

ELECTRIC GUITAR DIAGRAM

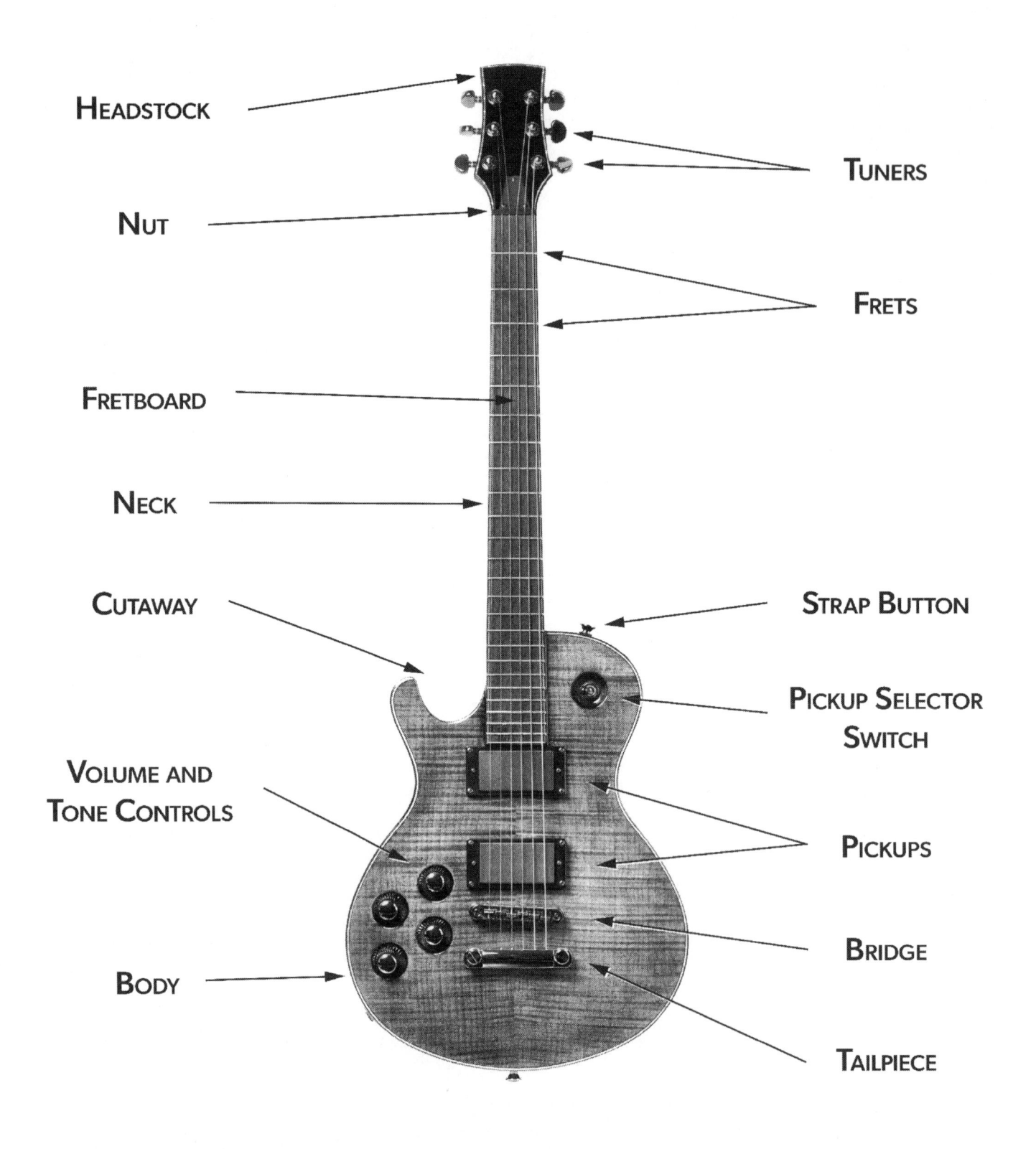

- **Headstock**
- **Tuners**
- **Nut**
- **Frets**
- **Fretboard**
- **Neck**
- **Cutaway**
- **Strap Button**
- **Pickup Selector Switch**
- **Volume and Tone Controls**
- **Pickups**
- **Bridge**
- **Body**
- **Tailpiece**

Fig.10 - Electric Guitar Features

12 ELECTRIC GUITAR FOR LEFT-HANDED ADULTS - BOOK 1 - SEEING MUSIC METHOD BOOKS

How to Read Chord Diagrams: A Beginner's Guide

CHORD DIAGRAMS ARE VISUAL REPRESENTATIONS THAT INDICATE HOW TO PLAY CHORDS ON THE GUITAR. THEY SERVE AS A ROADMAP FOR FINGER PLACEMENT ON THE FRETBOARD.

CHORD DIAGRAM BASICS

At first glance, a chord diagram looks like a grid. Think of it as a snapshot of the top part of your guitar neck.

- Nut (Thick line)
- Frets (Horizontal)
- Strings (Vertical.)

Vertical Lines: Each vertical line represents a string on your guitar. If you're playing a standard six-string guitar, there will be six vertical lines. From right to left, these lines represent the low E, A, D, G, B, and high E strings.

Horizontal Lines: These lines represent the frets on the guitar neck. The topmost line often indicates the nut of the guitar. In this book, a "0" is written beside the nut.

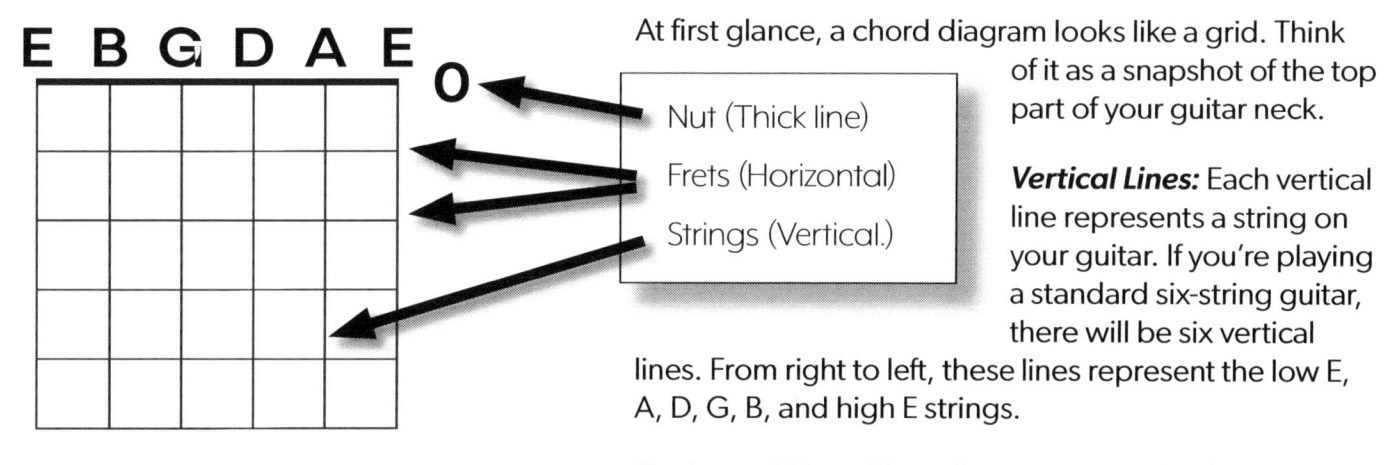

FIG.11 - OPEN-STRING NAMES

Black Dots: These dots tell you where to place your fingers. The placement of the dot corresponds to the location, string, and fret of your finger.

Numbers Inside Dots: Some chord diagrams will have numbers inside the dots. These numbers indicate which finger to use. (1 = index finger, 2 = middle finger, 3 = ring finger, 4 = pinky finger)

X's and O's: Above the diagram, you might see the shapes of "X" or "O" aligned with certain strings. An "X" means that you won't play that string. An "O" means you should play the string open, without adding any fret fingers.

X's
String is not used, don't play

Open Dots
Play the open-string

Black Dots
Place your fingers here

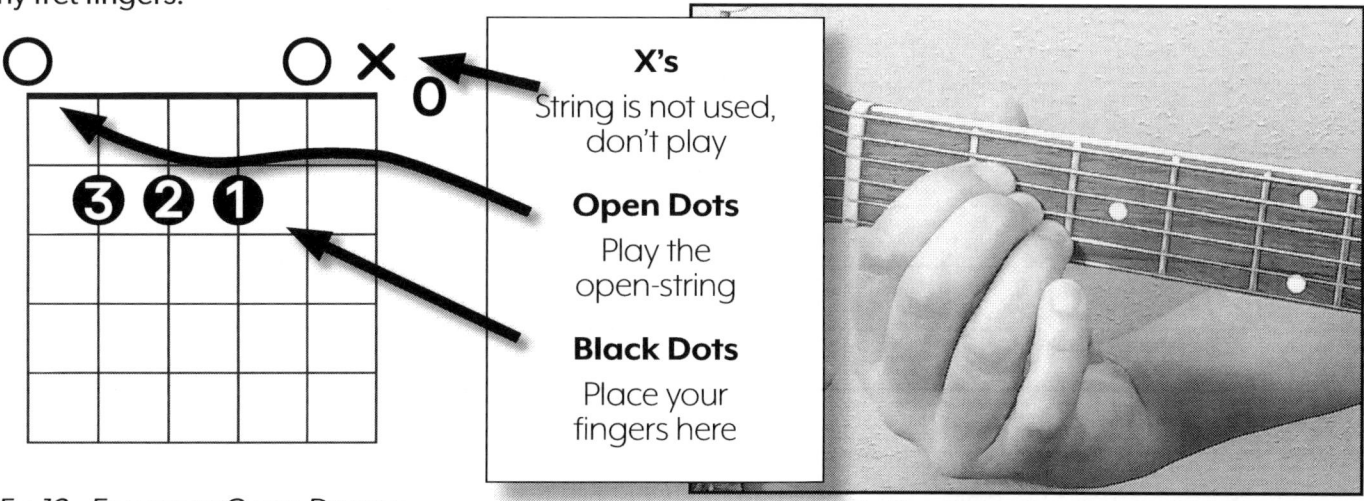

FIG.12 - EXAMPLE OF CHORD DIAGRAM

FIG.13 - FRET FINGER PLACEMENT - A MAJOR

HOW TO READ CHORD DIAGRAMS

HOW TO READ CHORD DIAGRAMS

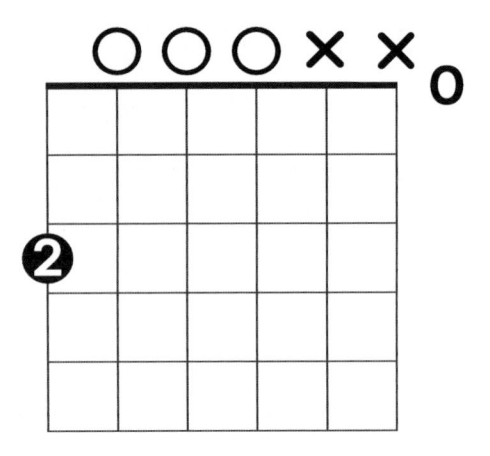

Fig.14 - Diagram - G Major Easy

Fig.15 - G Major Easy - Hand Position

1 Start by examining the chord diagram here, beginning with the bottom of the chord, the lowest pitched string. It's the 6th string E, which appears as the vertical line on the right. It corresponds to your lowest-pitched guitar string, the one furthest from the floor. In the chord here, G Major Easy, there is no black dot on the 6th string, only an X above it. An X over the string means the string is not played.

2 Check for any other X's or O's. X's indicate strings that aren't used, while O's mark open-strings. In this chord, strings 6 and 5 are not played, indicated by the X's over those strings. Strings 4, 3 and 2 are played open as indicated by the O's.

3 If the string has a black dot with a number, place your corresponding finger on that string near that fret. Read the number in the dot and use that finger. Placing your finger near the fret produces the best sound. In this chord, the 2nd finger presses at the 3rd fret. This is the 1st string, high E. It is your string closest to the ground.

4 Strum the chord to hear how it sounds. If you'd like to try this chord, don't forget to avoid strumming the 6th and 5th strings (marked by X's).

14 Electric Guitar for Left-Handed Adults - Book 1 - Seeing Music Method Books

PRACTICAL TIPS FOR READING CHORD DIAGRAMS

Orientation: Always ensure that you're viewing the chord diagram with the correct orientation. The vertical lines represent your guitar strings, with the line nearest the starting-fret number, corresponding to your low E string.

Barre Chords: In this book, barred fretting (when a finger is layed across the strings, playing multiple notes at once) are indicated by several dots, all with the same finger number inside them. Outside of this book, you might encounter a chord diagram displayed as a curved line across multiple strings. This indicates a barre chord, where one finger (usually the index) presses down on multiple strings simultaneously.

Chord Name: When sheet music contains chord charts, the name of the chord is typically written above the chord diagram. Not all sheet music has chord charts for guitar. Some charts have just the chord name. Familiarize yourself with common chord names like G Maj (G Major), Dmin (D minor), A7, C Maj7 (C Major 7). These are all found later in this book.

As you gain experience, you'll have these chords committed to memory and won't always need chord chart sheet music.

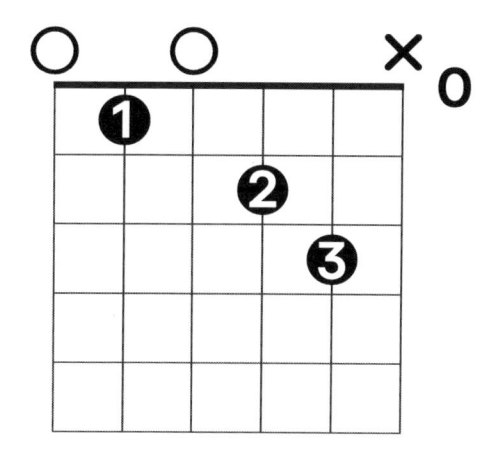

FIG.16 - C MAJOR - FULL

FIG.17 - C MAJOR - FULL HAND POSITION

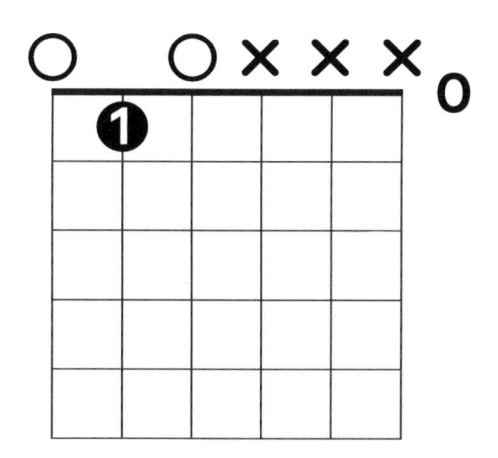

FIG.18 - C MAJOR - EASY

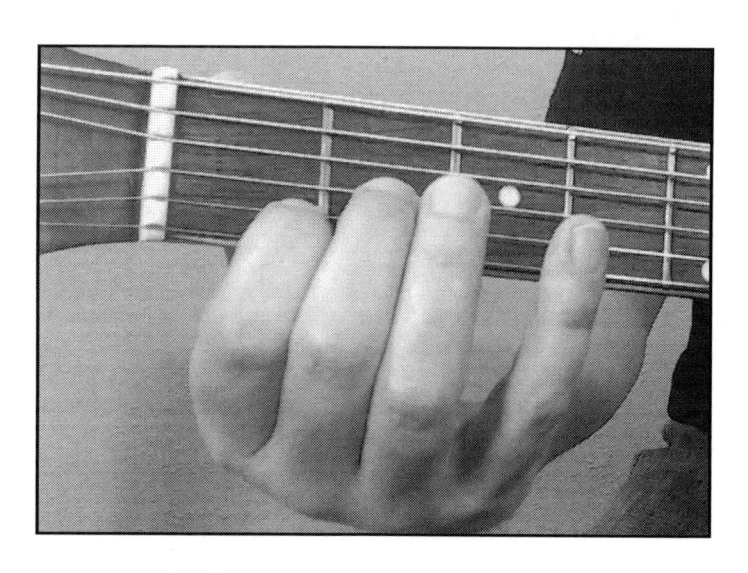

FIG.19 - C MAJOR - EASY HAND POSITION

HOW TO READ CHORD DIAGRAMS

LEARNING BONUS - MEMORIZE YOUR STRINGS

Elephants
And
Donkeys
Grow
Big
Ears

Be sure you memorize the names of your strings. Here's a quick way to easily remember them.

The strings of the guitar are, in order (Lowest to Highest): E, A, D, G, B and E

Just remember:
Elephants and Donkeys Grow Big Ears!

16 Electric Guitar for Left-Handed Adults - Book 1 - Seeing Music Method Books

ABOUT CHORD NAMES AND SYMBOLS

CHORD NAMES AND SYMBOLS ARE WRITTEN IN SEVERAL FORMS, WHICH CAN SOMETIMES MAKE LEARNING THEM PRETTY CONFUSING. HERE'S A WAY TO BREAK DOWN THOSE CHORD SYMBOLS AND GET THEIR MEANING, EVERY TIME.

Every chord has a root note and every chord has a flavor, such as Major or Minor. To keep the names simple, the flavor will often be omitted if the chord is Major. Instead of "C Major", you could just say "C".

Here you can see the most common ways to indicate a C Major chord and an A minor chord.

Notice that if real simplicity is needed, only one letter might be used. If major, the single letter abbreviation is capitalized. If the chord is minor, the single letter symbol is not capitalized. As with "C" and "a", shown in the figure.

C Cmaj C△

a Am Amin A⁻

Fig.20 - Chord Name Equivalents

To add more sonic color and variety, some chords use extensions. These additional notes build on the basic minor or major chord. The extension is awritten at the end of the chord symbol.

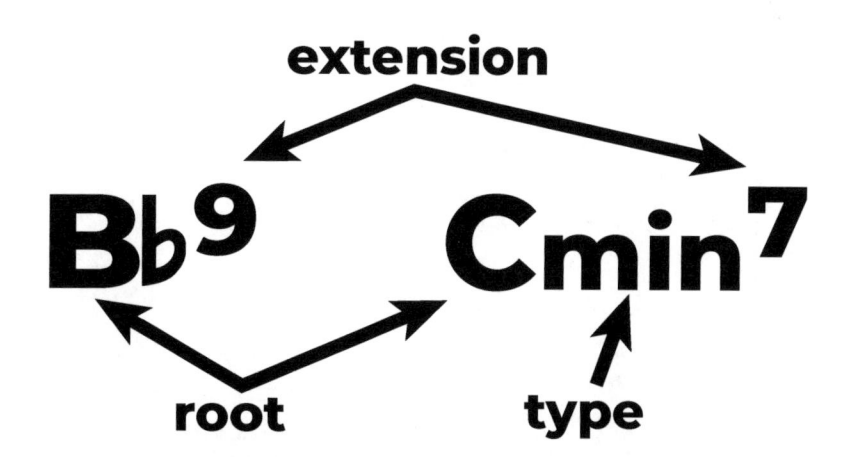

extension

B♭⁹   Cmin⁷

root   type

You'll be learning some extended chords later in this book. If you're curious about extensions and how to use them, check out *Guitar Theory Nuts and Bolts* from Seeing Music.

How to Read Chord Diagrams 17

How music fits together.
Scales, chords and songs.

See more music.
SeeingMusicBooks.com

Scan to learn more

SEEING MUSIC METHOD BOOKS

18 Electric Guitar for Left-Handed Adults - Book 1 - Seeing Music Method Books

Start at Square One: Play Single Notes Cleanly

GOOD ELECTRIC GUITAR WORK MEANS PLAYING CLEANLY AND ACCURATELY. BEFORE DIVING INTO WHOLE CHORDS, TAKE A MINUTE TO CHECK OUT YOUR NOTES INDIVIDUALLY.

PLAY JUST ONE NOTE

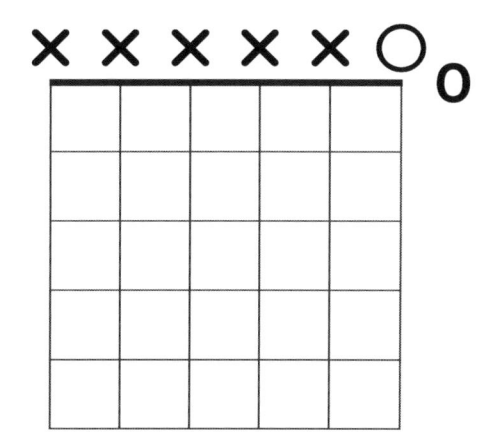

Fig. 21 - Open E

Remember the notes from the earlier lesson that acquainted you with the string names? Begin with your lowest-string, open E. With your left-hand thumb or a pick, play the open E on the 6th string. This is the biggest sounding note on your guitar and it's charged with lots of sonic energy.

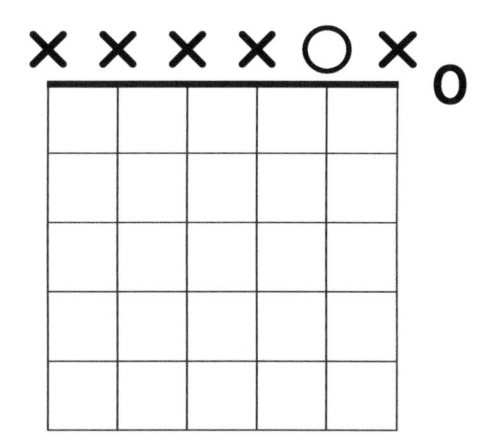

Fig. 22 - Open A

Next, focus on the open A. It's beneficial to glance at your picking hand to ensure you're precisely striking the 5th string. It's common to accidentally hit adjacent strings, so maintain precision to target just the A string.

PLAY SINGLE NOTES 19

FRETTING WITH PRECISION

HOLD YOUR GUITAR IN GOOD PLAYING POSITION. IF NECESSARY, REVISIT THE CHAPTER "FOUNDATIONS OF GUITAR PLAYING".

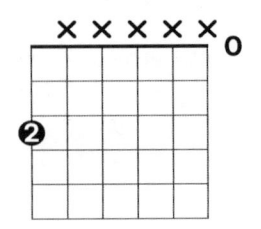

Fig.23 - 1st String - G

Fig.24 - 2nd String - D

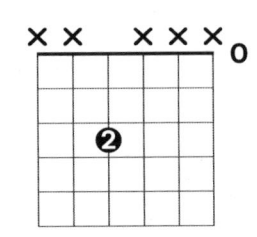

Fig.25 - 3rd String - B flat

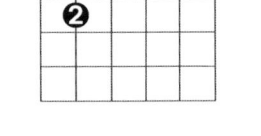

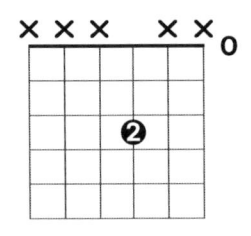

Fig.26 - 4th String - F

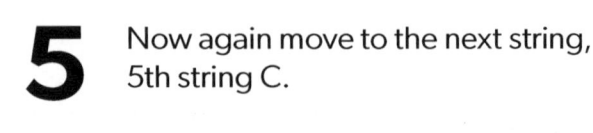

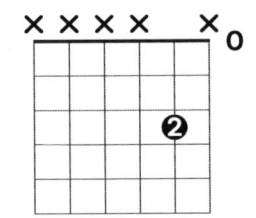

Fig.27 - 5th String - C

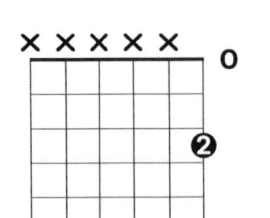

Fig.28 - 6th String - G

1 Starting with the 1st String (the one closest to the ground) find the 3rd fret. The nut is considered "0", the first fret is 1, then count 2, then 3. Place your finger between the 2nd and 3rd frets, very close to the 3rd. You should be right up against the fret, but not on top of it for the best sound. Play this note. It is the 1st String note, G.

2 You can release that note. Now similarly, The 2nd string's 3rd fret is the note D. Use your fretting hand's 2nd finger here, too.

3 Now, move your fretting finger over one string to the 3rd string. At the 3rd fret, play B-flat.

4 Again, moving over one string, play the 4th string F.

5 Now again move to the next string, 5th string C.

6 Finally, play the 6th string G.

Now, reset your finger to the 1st string and repeat these steps several times. Go slowly and accurately.

How does that sound? It's a very simple exercise, but an important one.

20 Electric Guitar for Left-Handed Adults - Book 1 - Seeing Music Method Books

PERFECT YOUR TONE

How's the resonance? Any unwanted buzzing? A rich, clear note is the aim. Most learners require consistent practice before achieving clean notes. If there are issues, ensure your finger is very close to the fret – almost on top of it. This positioning is vital and once mastered, simplifies later learning.

Keep your wrist straight by raising the neck and positioning the fretboard close to your shoulder. Always prioritize comfort—if you feel any discomfort or pain, stop right away. While fingertip soreness is normal for beginners, calluses will develop over time, making it easier to play.

STOPPING YOUR STRINGS

Notes have both a start and an endpoint. While starting a note is straightforward, there are two main ways to stop it. For example, play an open A, followed by an open E. Use your pick or thumb to start each note, and lightly touch the string with your fretting fingers to stop it. The same goes for fretted notes like C and G—simply release the pressure on the fret to silence them.

Another way to stop the string is by using your picking hand which is known as *palm muting*. It's like applying brakes on a car. After striking a note, gently rest the fleshy edge of your hand (between your pinky and wrist) on the strings to mute them. Try different speeds to see how it affects the sound.

> Notice the very, very subtle touch the side of the palm gives the strings when needing to stop their ringing.
>
> In the middle photo at right, there is a slight separation between the palm and strings.
>
> In the lower photo, the palm has lightly contacted the strings, muting them.

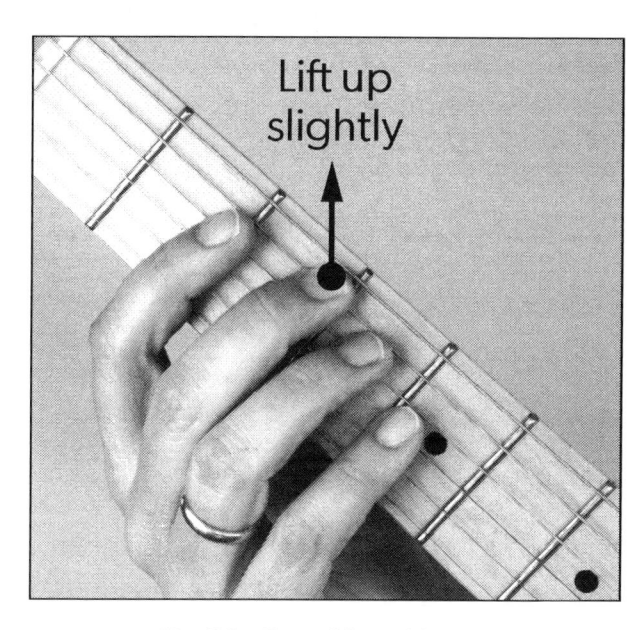

FIG. 29 - RIGHT-HAND MUTING

FIG. 30 - PICKING POSITION

FIG. 31 - PALM MUTING

PLAY SINGLE NOTES 21

UNDERSTANDING STAFF NOTATION

Musical staffs tell you how to count each measure (or *bar*) of the music. Here, a Treble Clef with a time signature is illustrated. The Treble Clef (a fancy or curly "G" shape) indicates the range of notes (Bass Clef notes are lower pitched), while the time signature guides counting. In 4/4 time, the musician counts "1, 2, 3, 4" and then repeats that counting for the next measure. The bottom number 4, signifies that quarter notes are what are being counted. If eighth notes are being counted, the number would be 8. If half notes, it is 2.

Fig.32 - 4/4 Time Signature

Think of each measure as a container that holds a <u>specific</u> number of musical notes or beats of a <u>specific</u> type. In the case of 4/4 time, there are 4 beats per measure (that's the top number) and each beat is a quarter note (that's the bottom number).

FAQ: Understanding Note Types and Rhythms

Whole note: Lasts for 4 beats. Just one fills an entire measure in 4/4 time.

Half note: Lasts for 2 beats. So, two half notes fill a measure in 4/4.

Quarter note: Lasts for 1 beat. You can fit four of these in one measure of 4/4.

Eighth notes: These are half the length of a quarter note, so they last for half a beat. It takes eight of these to fill a measure.

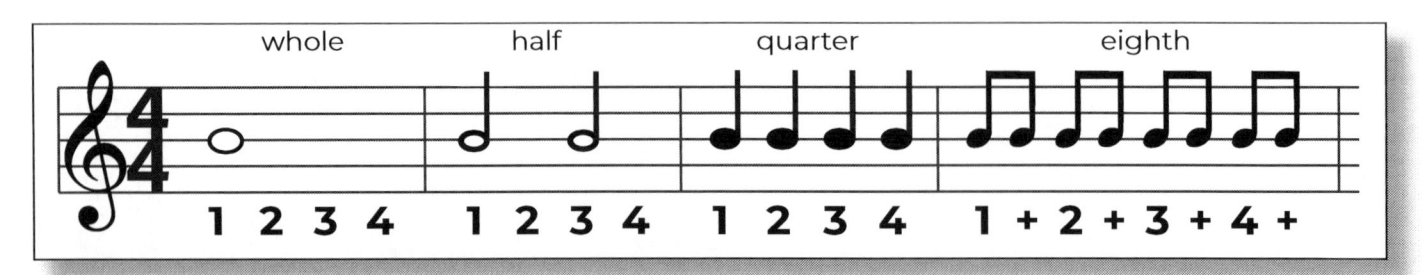

Fig.33 - Note Types

22 Electric Guitar for Left-Handed Adults - Book 1 - Seeing Music Method Books

Rests: Just like there are notes of different lengths, there are also rests of different lengths. Rests are moments of silence where no note is played, but they still take up space in our "container". So, if you see a rest, it means you don't play a note for that beat or beats, but you will count them in your rhythm.

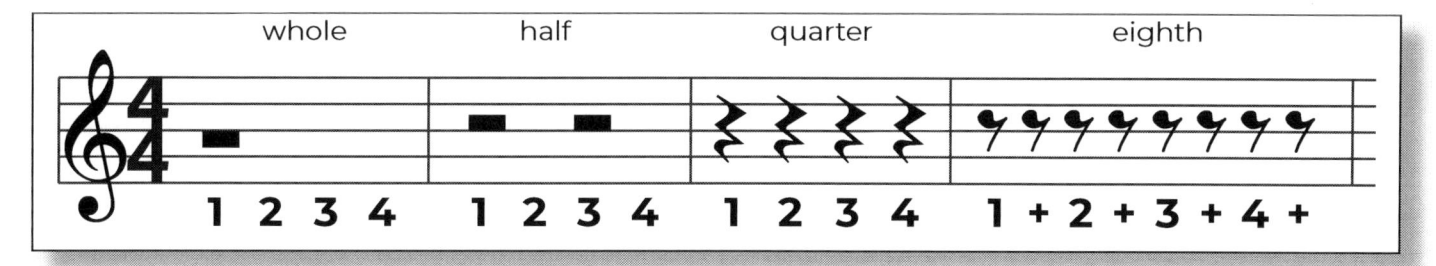

Fig. 34 - Various Rest Types

Notice how the half and whole rests look a lot alike? The whole rest hangs below the staff line; the half sits above it. Some students remember them this way: Whole notes resemble a hole in the ground, while the half-note looks a bit like a hat. "Half" sounds like "hat". Just remember "Whole rests are like holes, Halves are like Hats."

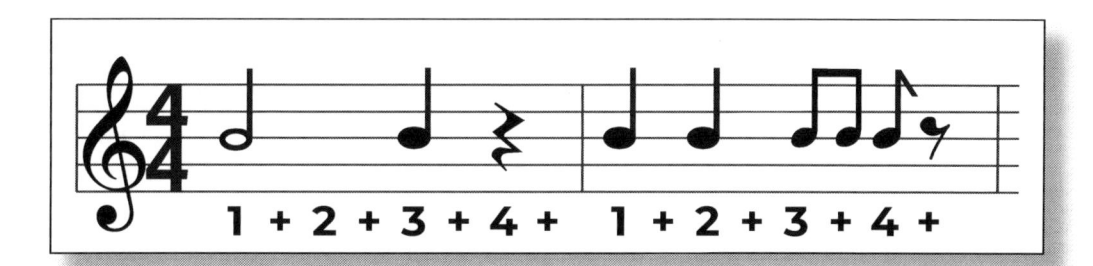

And most importantly, a measure can be filled with a mix of any of these note or rest types, as long as they total the number of beats indicated in the time signature.

Fig. 35 - Mixed Value Notes and Rests

Study the 2nd measure, beats 3 and 4. There are three eighth notes and one eighth rest. Sometimes eighth notes are tied together at the top, as in beat 3. Because only one eighth note is used in the fourth beat, the flag at the top of the eighth note is angled down.

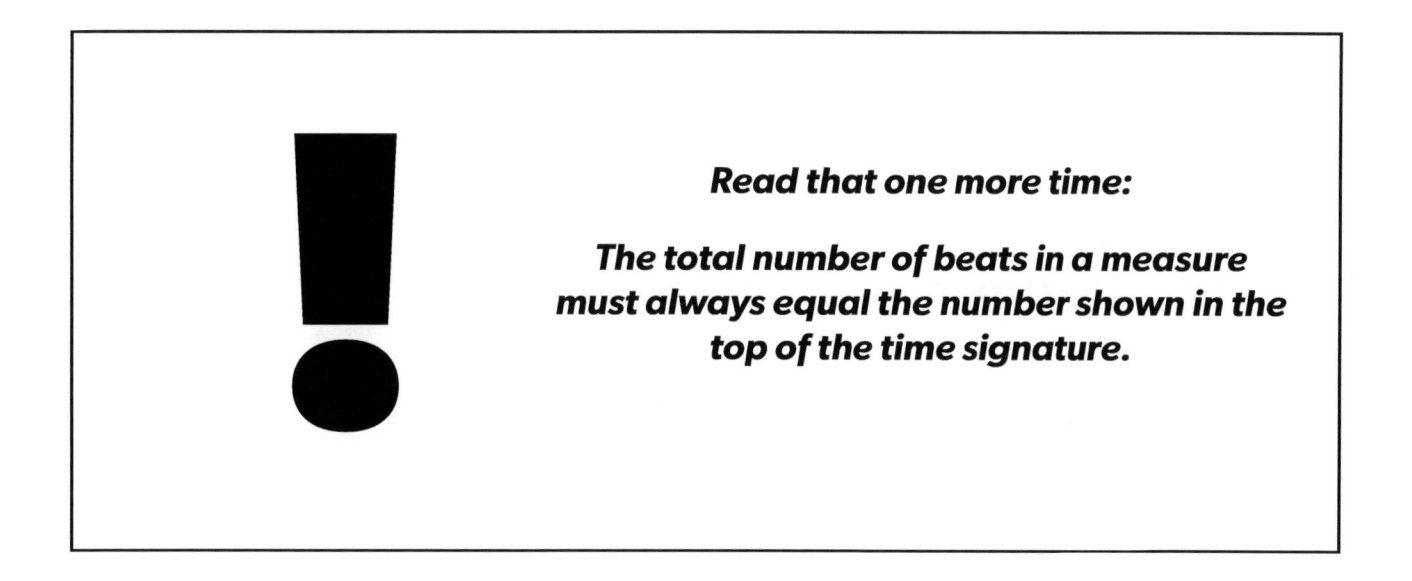

Read that one more time:

The total number of beats in a measure must always equal the number shown in the top of the time signature.

PLAY SINGLE NOTES 23

Reading and Playing Measures

When reading music with a 4/4 time signature:

1 Start at the beginning of the measure.

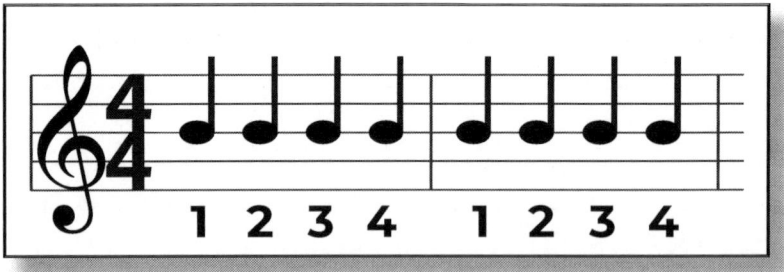

2 Count each beat as you play. You can softly count, "1, 2, 3, 4" to ensure you're giving each note or rest its proper length.

3 When you reach the end of one measure (after the 4th beat), move on to the next one and continue counting.

Fig. 36 - Two Measures of Quarter Notes

Subdividing Beats

Sometimes it's helpful to count rhythms with more precision than just "1, 2, 3, 4". For example, this measure of eighth notes is counted "1 and, 2 and, 3 and, 4 and". The "plus" sign is used when writing down "and".

Fig. 37 - One Measure of Eighth Notes

By understanding the 4/4 time signature and how beats are divided in a measure, you'll have a solid foundation to start reading and playing music. Just remember to keep counting and make sure everything adds up to 4 in each measure!

Fretting with Ease

Don't press too hard when fretting. It can cause notes to be "bent" out-of-tune and also causes unnecessary hand strain.

SINGLE-NOTE EXERCISES

Practice producing and then silencing notes. The staff's beats denote the moment to play the chord, which is stated above that measure.

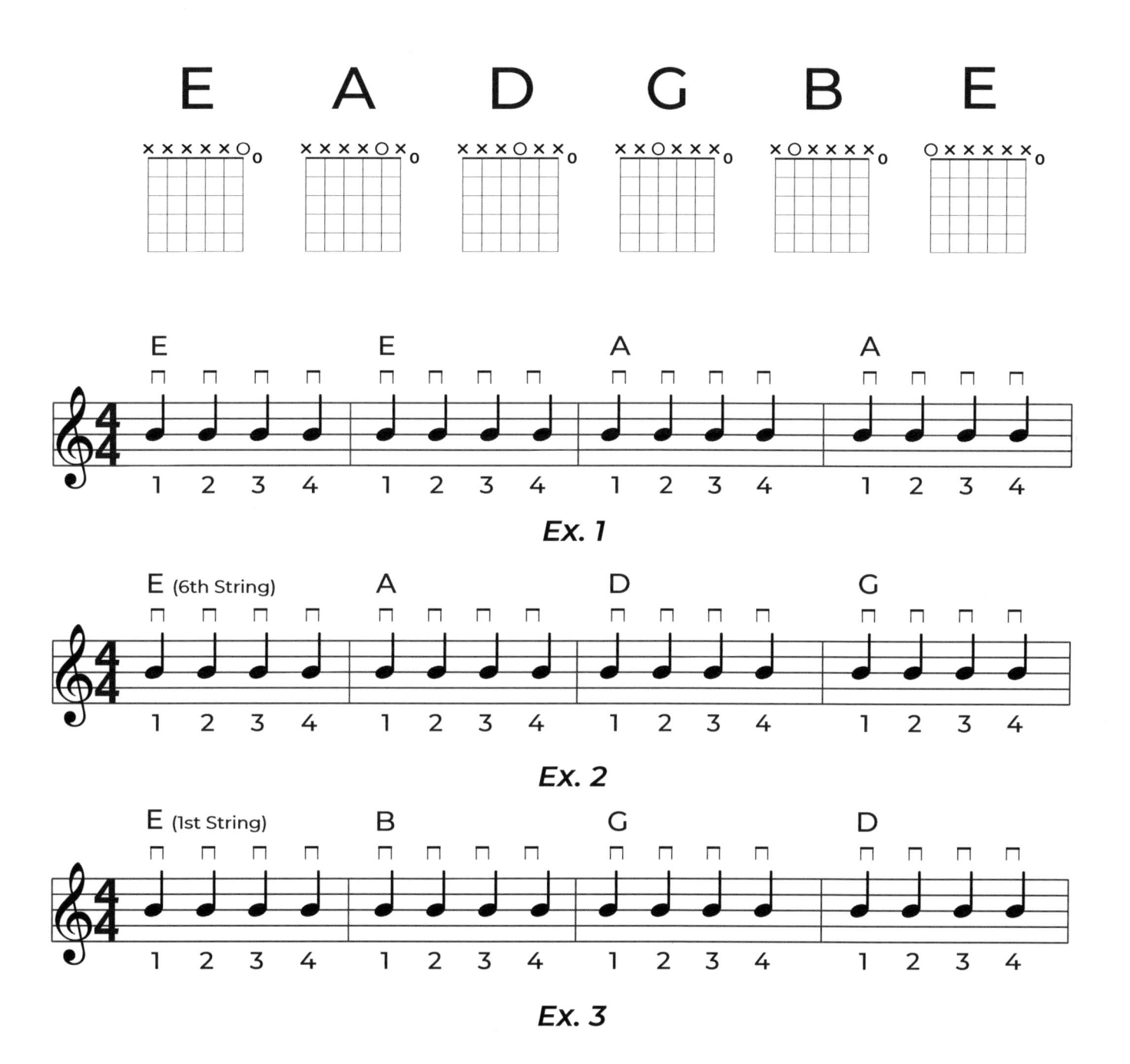

E A D G B E

Ex. 1

Ex. 2

Ex. 3

Note: Ordinarily, notes reside on various staff lines, indicating which note is to be played. In this book, the notes just show the rhythm, not the pitch. This is for simplicity while you're first learning.

G C F B♭ D G

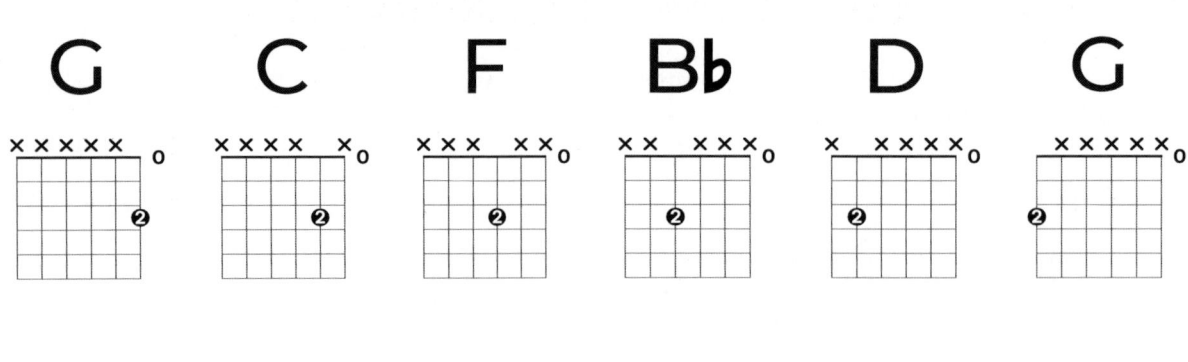

Ex. 4 — G (1st String) | D | B♭ | F

Ex. 5 — G (6th String) | C | F | G (1st String)

Ex. 6 — G (6th String) | C | G (6th String) | C

Ex. 7 — F | B♭ | D | B♭

26 Electric Guitar for Left-Handed Adults - Book 1 - Seeing Music Method Books

Mastering Your First Chords: G Major and C Major

TWO OF THE MOST OFTEN PLAYED CHORDS ARE G MAJOR AND C MAJOR. THEY ARE THE ESSENTIAL BUILDING BLOCKS FOR MANY SONGS.

Fig. 38 - G Major - Full

Fig. 39 - G Major - Full Hand Position

Notice that the dots on your guitar's neck are at the 3rd and 5th fret. Memorize this. It will come in very handy.

HOW TO PLAY G MAJOR

1 Begin by placing your 2nd finger on the 6th string, 3rd fret. The name of this note is G. It's the root of the G Major chord.

2 Keeping your finger there, add your 1st finger on the 5th string, 2nd fret.

3 The next few strings (4th, 3rd, and 2nd strings) are played open. This means they should ring freely, so be careful not to inadvertently mute them with your fretting hand.

4 Again holding your first two fingers where the are, add your 4th finger on the 1st string, 3rd fret.

5 Strum gently across all the strings, listening for clarity. Adjust your fingers if any note sounds muffled.

6 Repeat this exercise seval times, each time striking one string..at..a..time!

Does this chord seem too difficult right now? Turn the page to find an easier version.

G AND C MAJOR 27

G MAJOR - EASY VERSION

If you've got very small hands, or find the full version of G Major to be too difficult, you can always pull out this awesome one-finger equivalent.

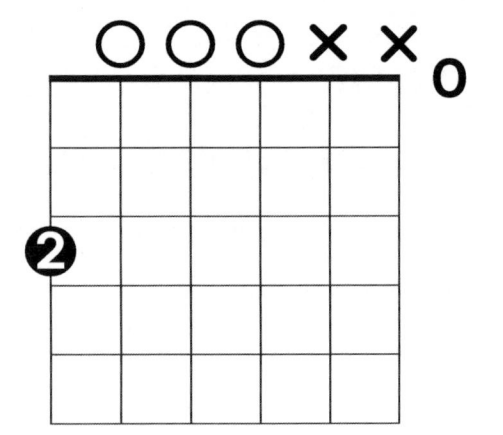

Fig. 40 - G Major - Easy

1 On the 1st string at the 3rd fret, place your 2nd finger Remember to keep it close to the 3rd fret.

2 With your pick or thumb, strum from the 4th string through the 1st. Avoid hitting the 5th and 6th strings.

Fig. 41 - G Major - Easy Hand Position

Exploring G Major

G Major has been a favorite for composers and songwriters alike due to its bright and full-bodied sound.

Congratulations, you just learned your first chord! G Major is probably the most used of all chords on the electric guitar. You'll be using this chord a lot.

HOW TO PLAY C MAJOR

1 Begin by pressing down on the 5th string, 3rd fret with your 3rd finger. This note is C, the root of C Major.

2 On the 4th string at the 2nd fret, add your 2nd finger.

3 Let the 3rd string ring open - no fingers needed here!

4 On the 2nd string at the 1st fret, place your 1st finger.

5 Ensure the 1st string is played open, allowing it to resonate clearly. Check to make sure your 1st finger is bent up and over this string.

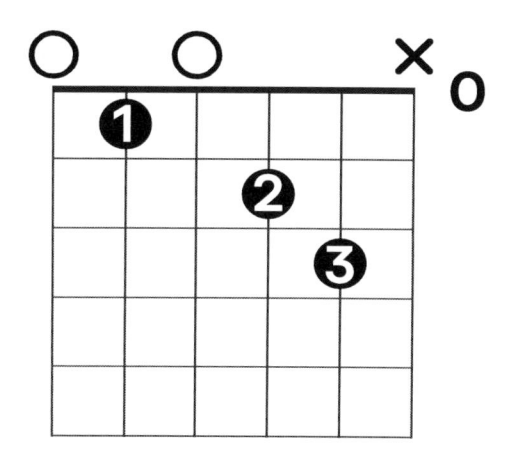

FIG.42 - C MAJOR - FULL

FIG.43 - C MAJOR - FULL HAND POSITION

When playing C Major, the 6th string isn't used. Be careful to not accidentally strum it. This takes practice.

How Guitar Became a Mainstay in Popular Music
The guitar became prominent in popular music in the 1950s with the rise of rock 'n' roll.

C MAJOR - EASY VERSION

One of the great things about the guitar is that there are **lots and lots** of ways to play any chord! Here's a super-simple version of C Major.

1 On the 2nd string at the 1st fret, place your 1st finger. Remember to keep it close to the 1st fret.

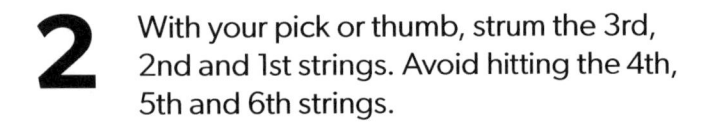

2 With your pick or thumb, strum the 3rd, 2nd and 1st strings. Avoid hitting the 4th, 5th and 6th strings.

And that's it! A super-simple, one-note C Major that sounds great, too.

G Major and C Major sound terrific together, which is why they're found in so many songs.

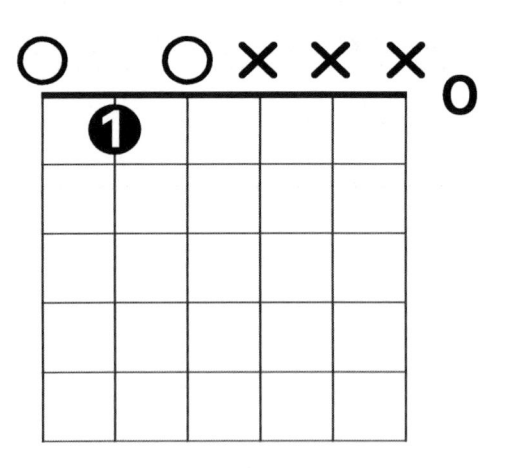

Fig.44 - C Major - Easy

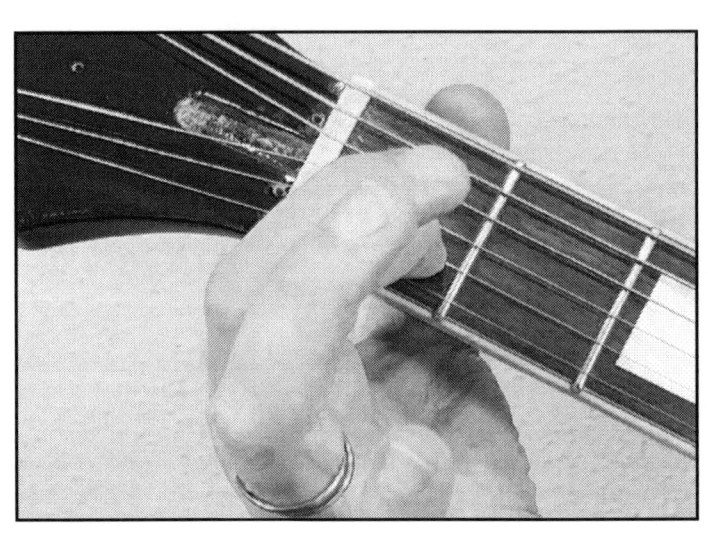

Fig.45 - C Major - Easy Hand Position

TROUBLESHOOT YOUR FRETTING HAND

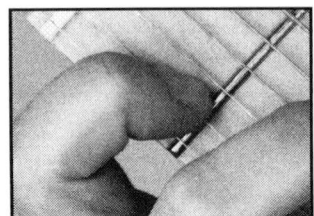

GETTING STUCK? HERE'S HOW TO IMPROVE YOUR TECHNIQUE.

Watch your finger posture. Your fingertips should be almost perpendicular to the fretboard, not slanting or resting lazily. Guitar strings are pretty close together and it's easy to accidentally touch two strings with the same finger.

Keep your fingers very close to the frets. This takes a little experimentation. Keeping your fingers near the frets improves the sustain and tone of the note.

How to find the problem finger: Starting with the lowest string of your chord, pick each string slowly and one-at-a-time. If your fret hand is in the correct position, you'll each each note ring clearly without stopping early, sounding muted or buzzing.

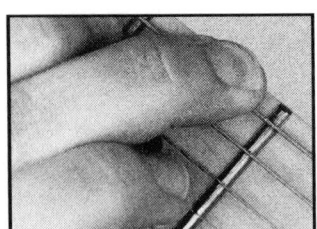

30 Electric Guitar for Left-Handed Adults - Book 1 - Seeing Music Method Books

EXERCISES FOR G AND C CHORDS

NOW THAT YOU'VE LEARNED THE BASICS, IT'S TIME TO CONNECT THE CHORDS AND PLAY SOME MUSIC!

In the following progressions, you'll read from left-to-right. Whole-notes (big circles with no stem) are played on count 1 and then held all four counts. Whole notes get four counts, half-notes (the circle notes with stems sticking up) receive two counts. Play very slowly at first and keep your eye on the changing chord name.

In the 4th example, the new symbol is a quarter-rest. Like a quarternote, it also has a one-count length, but it is silent, not strummed.

(Note: If you're used to reading music, disregard the note of the staff on which the notes sit. They just mark when to play the given chords.)

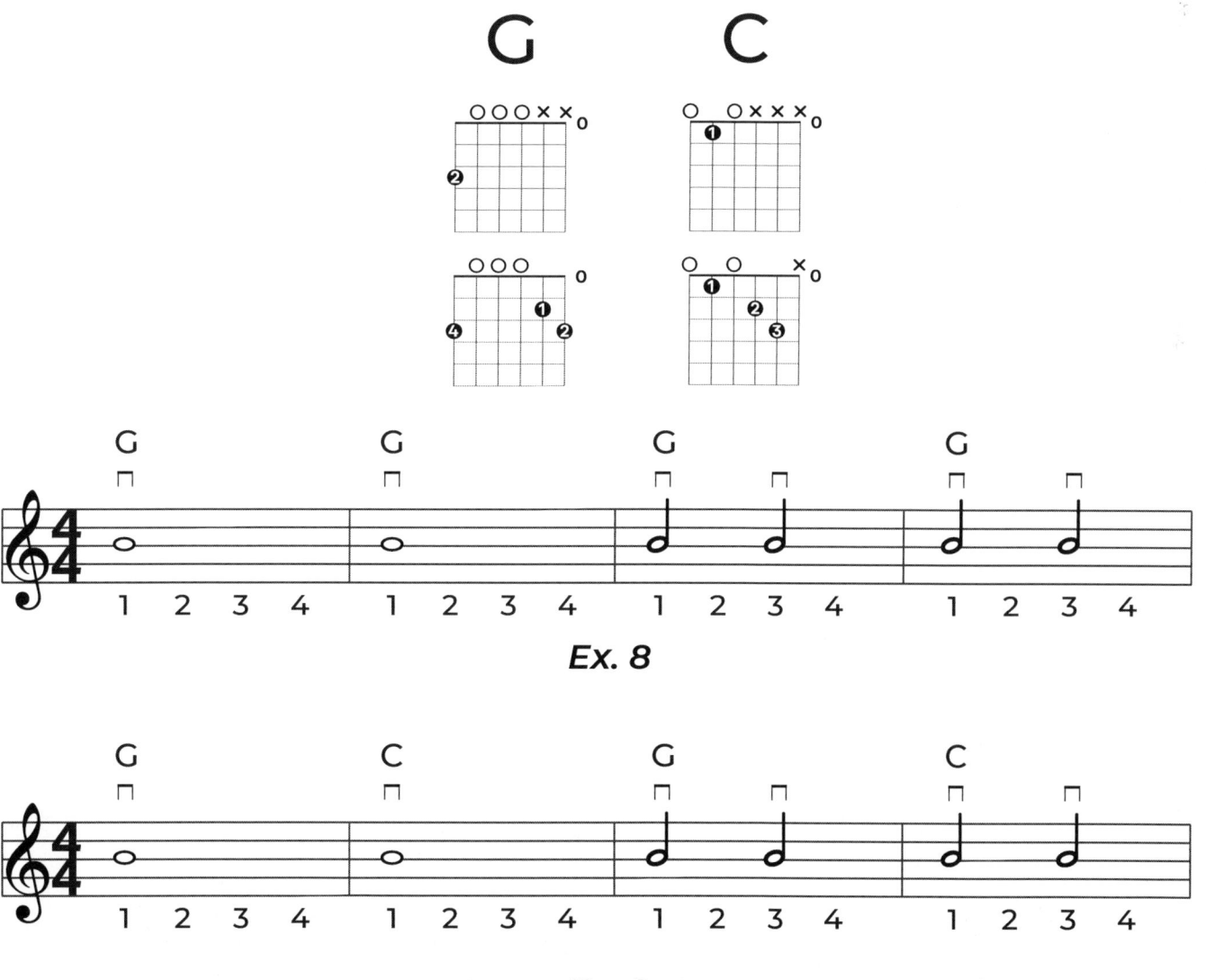

Ex. 8

Ex. 9

G AND C MAJOR

G   C

Practice these sequences slowly and before you know it, you'll be on your way to playing full songs. Remember, patience and practice are the keys to mastering the guitar. Happy strumming!

Ex. 10

Ex. 11

Ex. 12

Quarter Rest: Silence for 1 Count

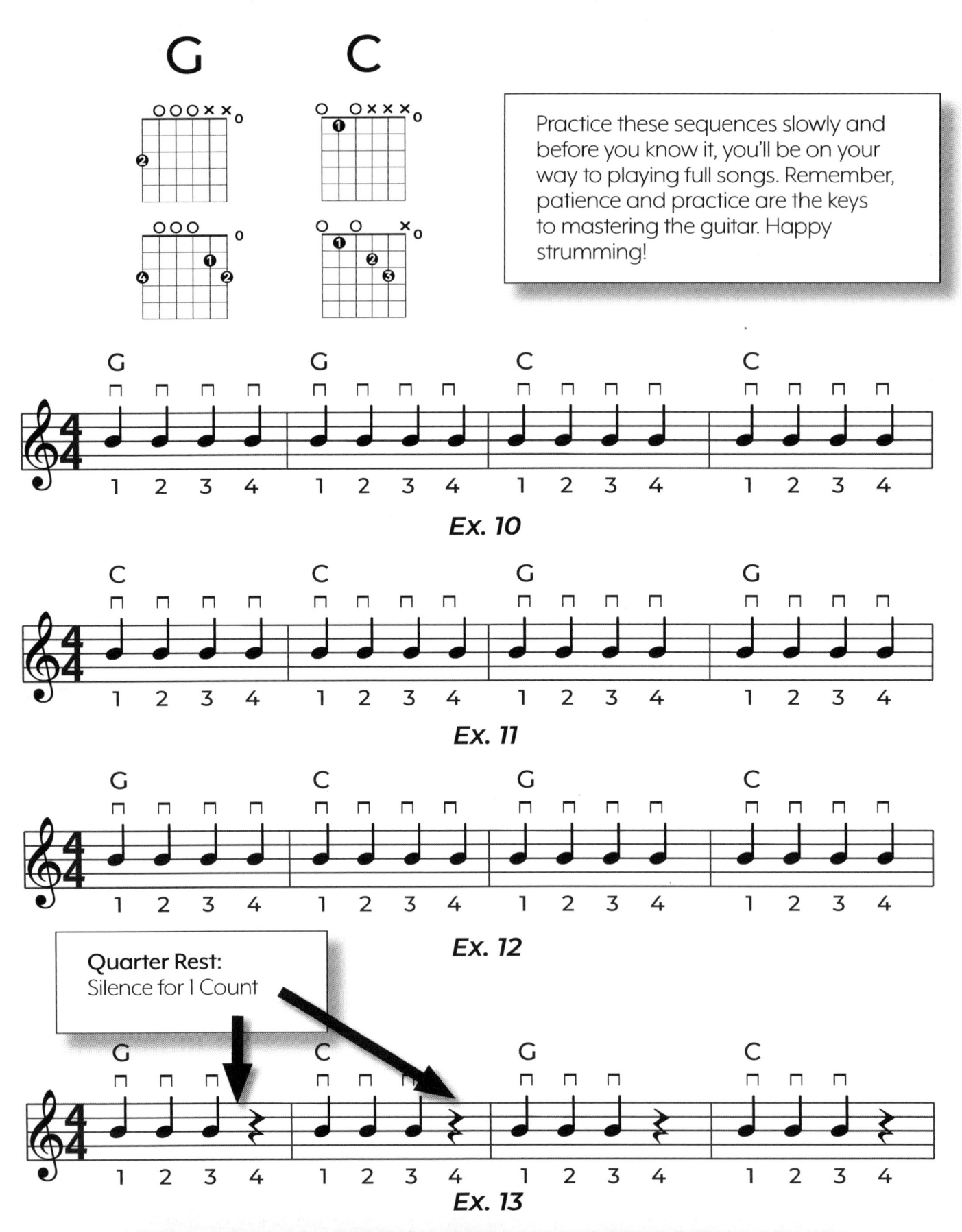

Ex. 13

How do these chords feel? Difficult? Strange? Like you need longer fingers? Every student feels this way at first. With practice, it gets much easier.

32 Electric Guitar for Left-Handed Adults - Book 1 - Seeing Music Method Books

Essential Knowledge: D Major

D MAJOR IS AN ESSENTIAL CHORD FOR GUITARISTS. USED UNIVERSALLY, IT HAS A UNIQUE PLACE IN EVERY GUITARIST'S TOOLKIT.

HOW TO PLAY D MAJOR USING 3 FINGERS

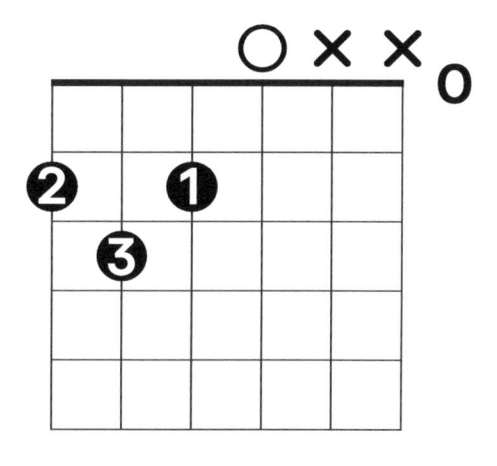

Fig.46 - D Major - Full

Begin by studying the D Major chord. You'll see that its root note is the open 4th string, which is D.

1 Start your finger placements with your 1st finger on the 2nd fret of the 3rd string.

2 Next, place your 3rd finger on the 3rd fret of the 2nd string.

3 Complete the chord by placing your 2nd finger on the 2nd fret of the 1st string.

4 When you strum, ensure you only play strings 1 through 4, avoiding the 6th and 5th strings to maintain the chord's integrity.

Fig.47 - D Major - Full Hand Position

When compared to many of the chords you'll learn in this book, D Major sounds a little less full and has a little less volume. That's because it doesn't use the 5th or 6th strings which are more bass-heavy. That's not bad, it just makes D Major a little different.

D MAJOR 33

D MAJOR - BARRE VERSION

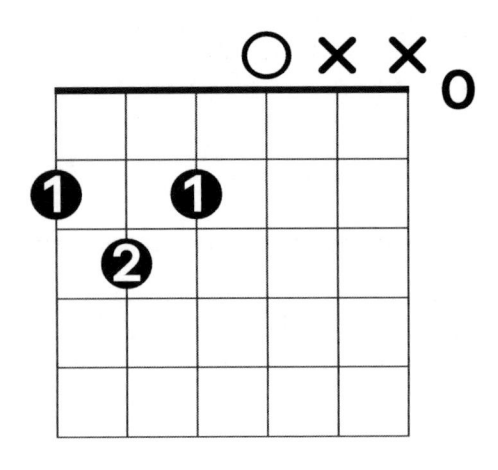

Fig. 48 - D Major - Barre Version

Many students find the conventional way of playing D Major with three fingers to be very difficult. Another way only uses two fingers. Depending on your personal preference, this may be an easier way. Use whichever method you prefer.

1 Play the open 4th string, D.

2 Place your 1st finger on the 2nd fret of the 3rd String.

3 Add your 2nd finger on the 3rd fret of the 2nd string.

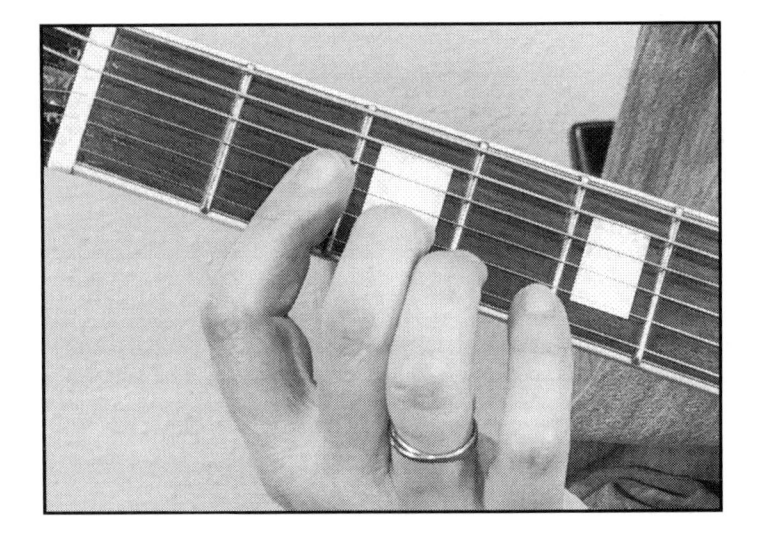

Fig. 49 - D Major - Barre Hand Position

4 Lay your 1st finger across all three strings, 1 through 3. The tip will remain on the 2nd string and the middle part of your finger will depress the 1st string at the 2nd fret.

5 When you strum, ensure you only play strings 1 through 4, avoiding the 6th and 5th strings.

> Throughout this book, the traditional chord fingering is referred to often. However, feel free to use whichever D Major chord fingering you find easier and more comfortable.

34 Electric Guitar for Left-Handed Adults - Book 1 - Seeing Music Method Books

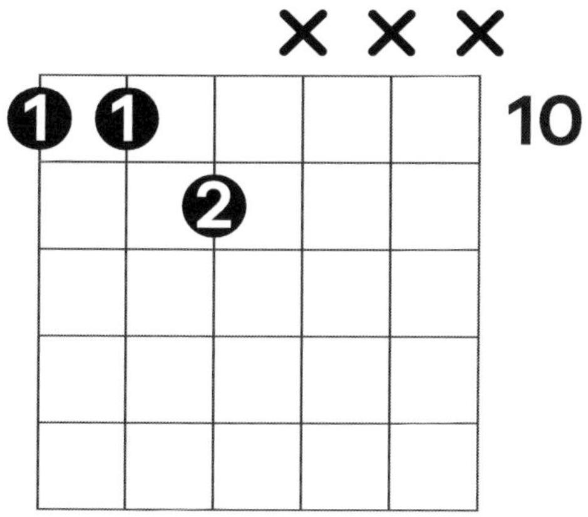

D MAJOR - EASY VERSION

Fig.50 - D Major - Easy

1 The number "10" in this chord diagram lets you know it is way up the neck. Ready to go? First, find your 10th fret.

2 Start your finger placement with your 2nd finger. On the 3rd string, at the 11th fret, hold it down now.

3 Next, put your 1st finger tip on the 2nd string at the 10th fret. Roll it down, so it's barre holding down both the 2nd and 1st strings.

4 When you strum, only play strings 3 through 1, avoiding the 4th, 5th and 6th strings.

Fig.51 - D Major - Easy Hand Position

Everyone Loves D Major!
D Major is known for its bright and triumphant sound.

The Origins of the Fretboard
The fretboard with raised frets is believed to have originated in the Middle East before spreading to Europe.

EXERCISES FOR D MAJOR

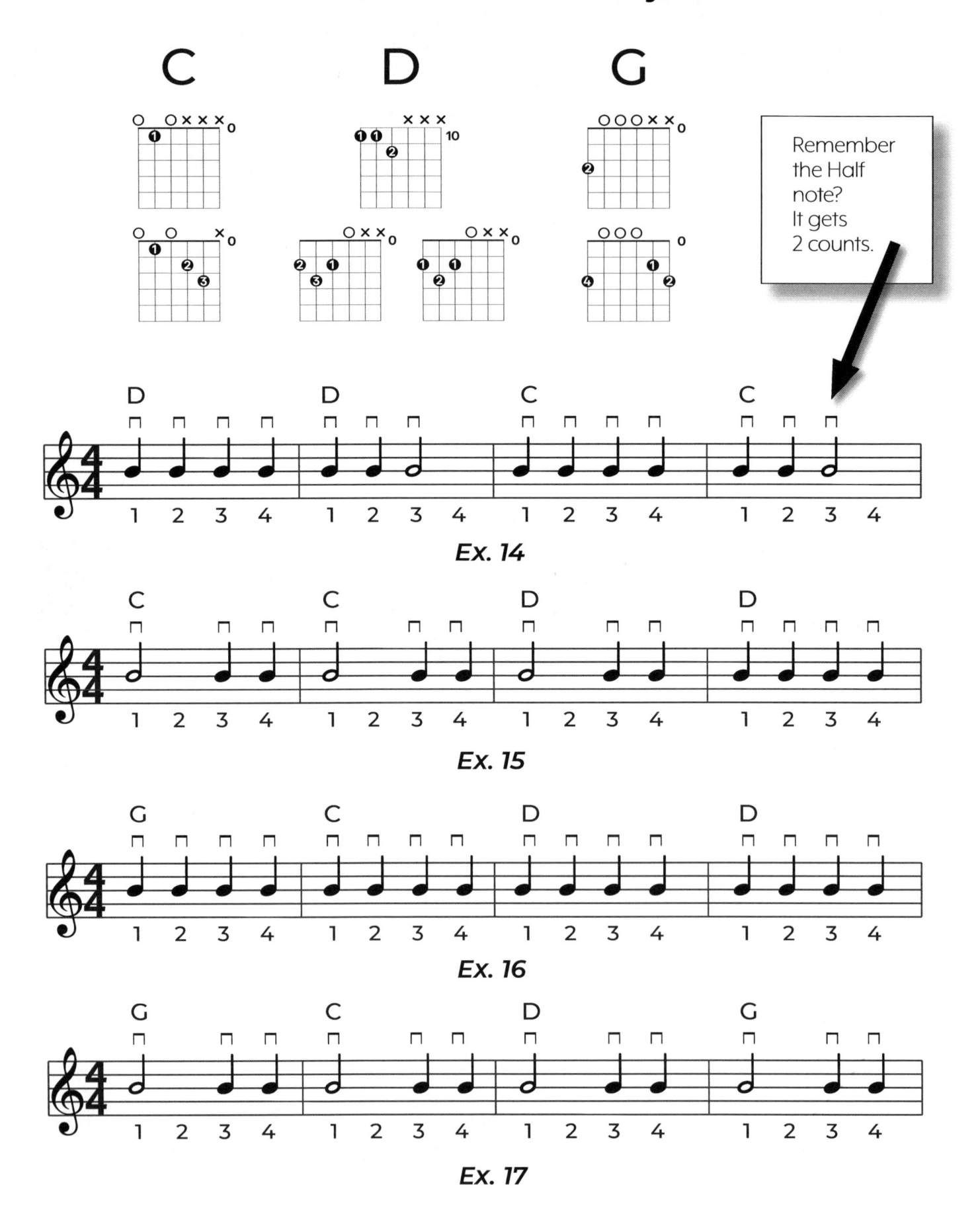

Ex. 14

Ex. 15

Ex. 16

Ex. 17

> Remember the Half note? It gets 2 counts.

Basic Strumming

THE 3 PARTS OF MUSIC ARE MELODY, HARMONY OR RHYTHM. STRUMMING ADDS RHYTHM AND AN OPPORTUNITY FOR VARIETY.

STRUMMING BASICS: JUST DOWN AND UP

Strumming involves two fundamental motions: the downstroke and the upstroke. Think of it as a continuous loop; for every downstroke, there will be a subsequent upstroke to bring your hand back to the starting point.

Start by practicing this motion without producing any sound. Simply move your strumming hand in a down, up pattern above the strings without making contact. This helps you get accustomed to the rhythm and movement.

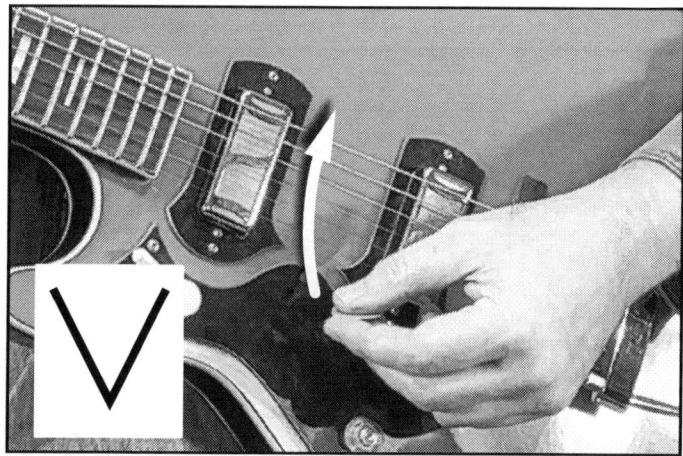

FIG. 52 - DOWNSTROKE

FIG. 53 - UPSTROKE

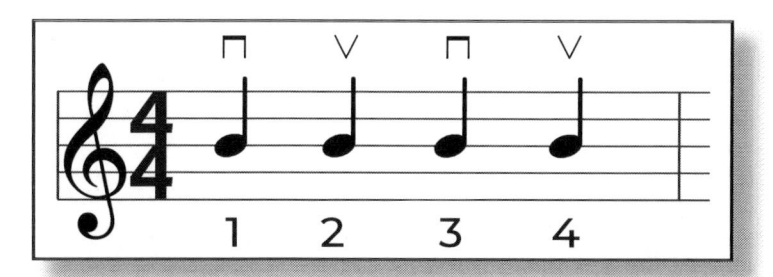

These marks indicate a Downstroke on beats 1 and 3, Upstroke on 2 and 4.

They read: "Down, Up, Down, Up."

BASIC STRUMMING 37

STRUMMING WORKSHOP: G MAJOR

GRAB A METRONOME AND SET IT TO 50 BPM FOR THIS RHYTHM-BUILDING WORKOUT. USE EITHER OF THE G MAJOR CHORDS BELOW.

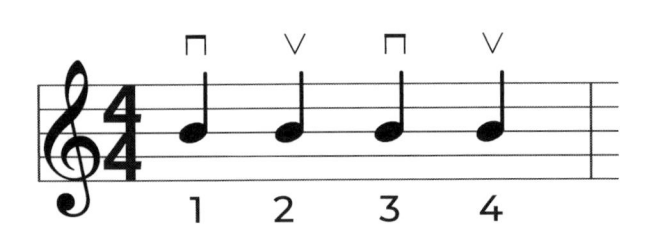

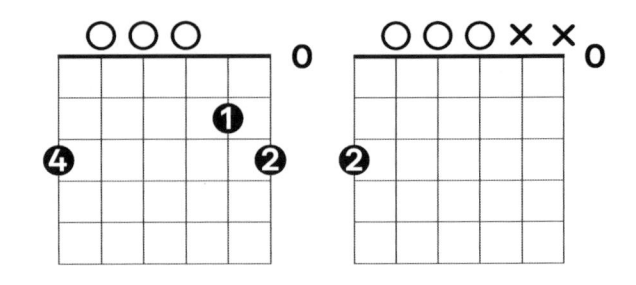

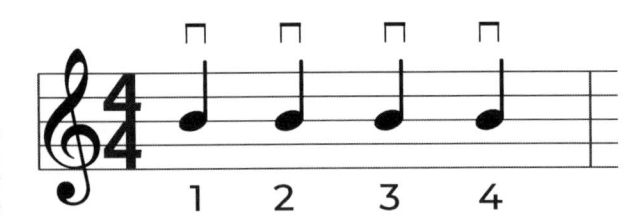

1 Strum the pattern shown. On every count of "1" and "3", you'll strum downward (toward the floor) and on "2" and "4", you'll strum the strings upward, as shown by the down- and upstroke marks over each beat.

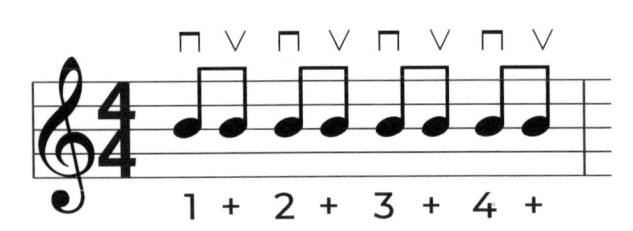

2 Now switch to downstrokes on all four beats.

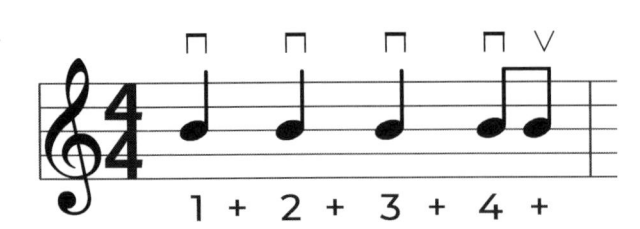

3 Add the upstrokes. These are eighth-notes, counted "One, -and, Two, -and..." Strum downward on the beat, upward on the "-and".

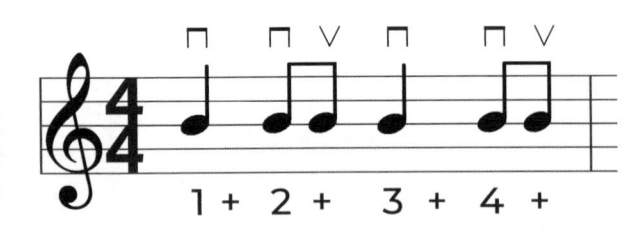

4 Put it all together for this combo rhythm! Use downstrokes on beats 1, 2 and 3. Play the fourth beat with a downstroke and upstroke on the "-and".

5 One more combo: Downstrokes on beats "1" and "3", down- and up- on "2 +" and "4 +".

38 ELECTRIC GUITAR FOR LEFT-HANDED ADULTS - BOOK 1 - SEEING MUSIC METHOD BOOKS

STRUMMING WORKSHOP: E MAJOR

Strumming adds rhythm and energy to your music. Rhythm adds variety and keeps things interesting.

Next, position your right hand to play an E Major chord.

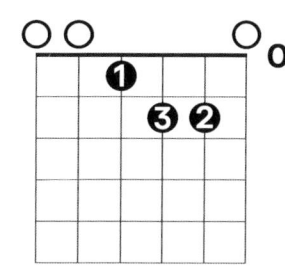

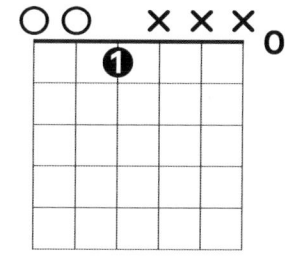

E Major Chords

With this chord held down, try the eighth-note strumming pattern, emphasizing both the down and up movements equally.

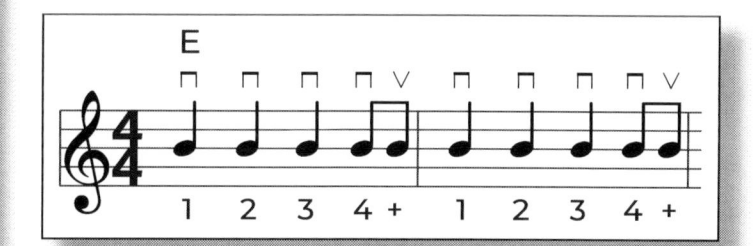

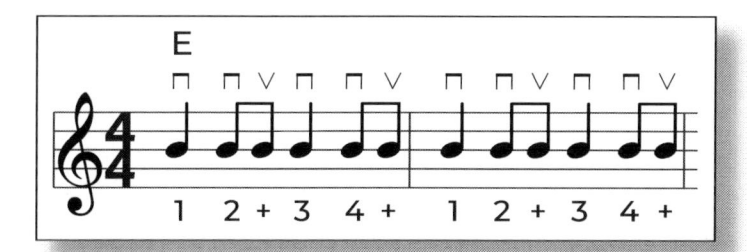

This rhythm you're practicing is based on eighth-notes. Two eighth-notes are equal to one quarter-note.

From Elvis to Modern Pop: The Evolution of Rhythm Guitar

Rhythm guitar techniques have evolved over the decades, from Elvis's straightforward rock 'n' roll rhythms to the more intricate, syncopated patterns heard in today's pop music.

BASIC STRUMMING 39

It's MUCH more than just a dictionary.

Fast Reference for Many Scales and Modes
Organized by Root and Scale Type
Multiple Fingerings for Each Scale
Learn to Spell Common and Exotic Scales
Learn Modes, Pentatonics and More

SEEING MUSIC METHOD BOOKS

Fast Reference for the Scales You Need in Every Key

LEFT-HANDED GUITAR
SCALES
ENCYCLOPEDIA

ANDY SCHNEIDER

BEGINNER TO ADVANCED

Scan to learn more

See more music at
SeeingMusicBooks.com

SEEING MUSIC METHOD BOOKS

40 Electric Guitar for Left-Handed Adults - Book 1 - Seeing Music Method Books

Setting Up Amps and Effects
INTRODUCTION TO AMPLIFIERS

CHARACTER, TEXTURE, AND THE ESSENCE OF YOUR SOUND.

Amplifiers and effects contribute a huge amount to the overall tone of an electric guitar. Some have

UNDERSTANDING YOUR AMP AND EFFECTS IS VERY IMPORTANT. IT'S NOT JUST ABOUT VOLUME; IT'S ABOUT

said they are the biggest factors determining the final sound. With that in mind, you'll want to really understand your equipment and it's contribution to your sound.

Amplifiers and effects both can affect the overall EQ of your sound. EQ affects the lows, mids and high frequencies of your sound. Both amplifiers and effects can also affect the **gain** of your sound. But what in the world is that? Gain?

Gain refers to how much amplification is happening inside a given device. Your electric signal starts very soft at your pickups and is amplified several times by various parts of your signal chain. This can lead to **distortion**, either intentionally or unintentionally. Distortion is a great name for what happens: your guitar signal becomes distorted from its original, crisp, clean sound. It might sound fuzzy or crunchy, like a car stereo playing way too loudly. Distortion happens any time a gain device approaches its electrical production limit. Think of those little circuits as being like a glass of water: You can fill it up to the top, but you can't overfill the glass. Distortion is usually caused by filling up those little circuits with more electricity than they can handle.

In the early days of electric guitar, distortion was considered something to be avoided. Then some creative guitarists started distoring their amps by playing a little too loud. It sounded good! Today, there are all kinds of amps that are designed and meant to be distorted and effects pedals that simulate that sound, too.

One thing is for certain: Once you've distorted part of your signal chain, you can't "un-distort" it. Clean sounds can be made dirty (distorted), but dirty sounds can't be made clean again. So, it helps to understand each component of your equipment and recognize which parts cause distortion so you can control it to your liking.

Here's a good method for adjusting your tone.

Turn off all effects: Set the amp for the clean tone you like. Start with all your amp's knobs (bass, mid, treble, volume) to the halfway point.

Adjust to Taste: From there, adjust to find a clean, clear sound. A clean tone should sound crisp and articulate.

SETTING UP AMPS AND EFFECTS 41

Fig.54 - Amp EQ Controls

Setting Amp Gain and Distortion

Gain Control: Slowly increase the gain or drive until you find a level of distortion that suits your style. There may be several knobs on your amp that make the whole amp louder and produce distortion at the same time. On some amps there is a Preamp gain knob, one for Power Amp gain, and one called something like "Distortion" or "Overdrive" Check your owners manual if you've got more than one knob for volume as the balance between the final volume and gain (leading to distortion) is very subtle. For example, if you have an amp with separate controls for the Preamp and the Power amp sections, you'll find that both can make the amp louder and both can also make it more distorted. You'll also notice a difference in the type of distortion. Distortions from preamps generally sound more "ground up finely", like a pepper shaker set to a really fine grind. Power amp distortion sounds much more coarse and gravel-like.

Balancing Volume: Ensure your volume level is consistent as you switch between clean and dirty settings. Sometimes amps come with channel switching, which allows you to set up both a clean sound and a dirty one and choose between them with just a switch.

Tailor Your Amp's EQ

Equalization (EQ) affects the balance of frequencies. Bass controls the low end, mid controls the middle frequencies, and treble controls the high end. Older amps may have just one tone knob that controls the general EQ all at once.

Adjusting EQ: Tweak the EQ settings while playing. Notice how each adjustment changes your sound.

If you want to experiment playing with high-gain (lots of distortion), try decreasing your mids or low-mids, if you have the amp controls. This is called an **EQ scoop** and it really helps clean up high-gain sounds by reducing the mids which tend to become too pronounced with gain.

Don't Ignore Your Tone Knob! Seriously, the tone knob is one of the least understood and most needed controls for a guitarist. Generally, you'll probably enjoy leaving it at full-on, or on 10. But as you experiment with more gain, try reducing that setting a bit. The more gain, the more you may want to roll that knob off. It reduces the "clicky" sound of the pick and frets which can make playing sound clumsy.

Using Effects

Many amps come with built-in effects like reverb and chorus. These can add depth and space to your sound.

If you're using an effects pedal, your guitar will plug into its input jack. Then you'll plug the pedal's output into the next pedal, or your amp's input. Be careful to always turn off your amp or put it on Standby when re-patching your cables to avoid speaker-blowing pops and clicks.

You can also chain several pedals together to create unique and highly creative pedal chains to tailor your sound. If you do, consider buying a good power supply which converts AC electricity into DC. Larger power supplies have several 9 volt DC outputs, one for each of your pedals. A good power supply is worth considering, not only for convenience, but it will save you from buying a ton of batteries.

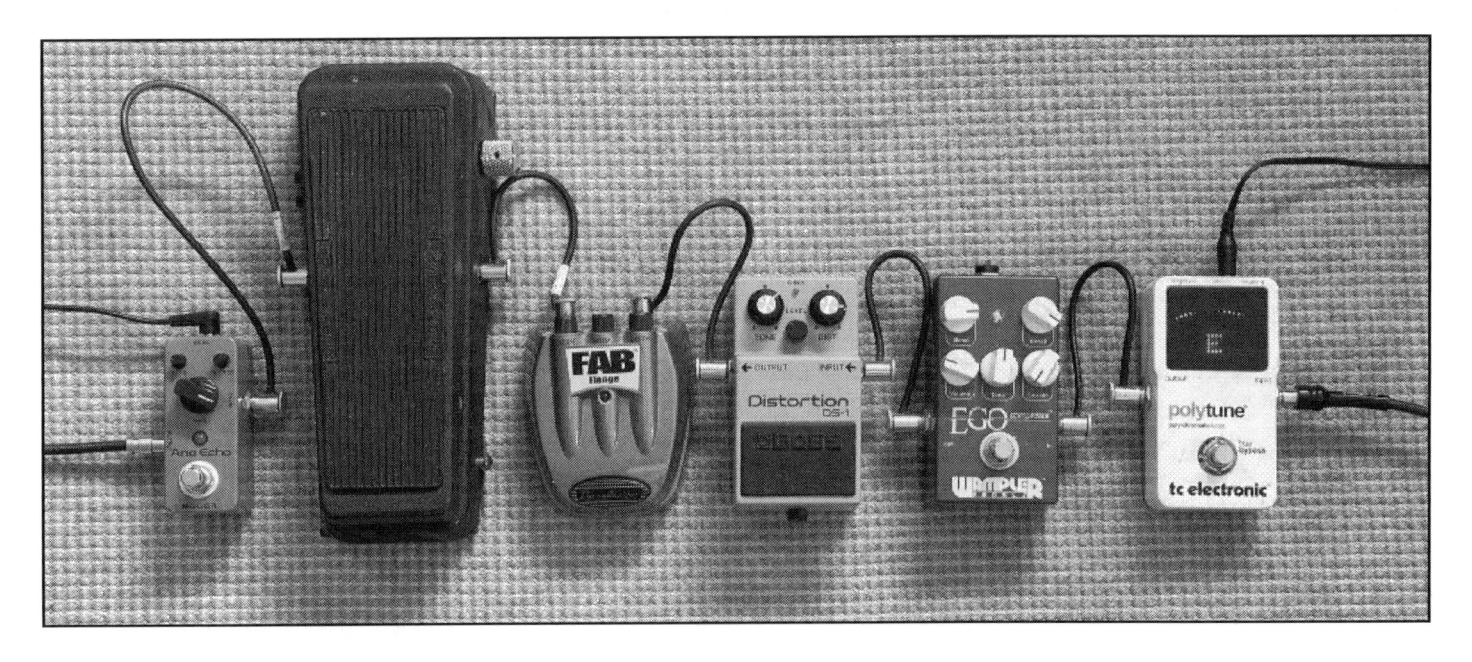

Fig.55 - Effects Pedal Chain

Standard Pedal Chain Order

While the order of effects is largely a matter of personal taste, this order is a good place to start your experimentation. From first to last:

Tuner: Putting your pedal tuner first avoids "confusing" the tuner with distortion or modulation effects.

Dynamics: Place compressors here.

Gain: Follow with overdrive or distortion.

Modulation: Chorus, phasers and flangers go here.

Wah-wah: While some prefer to put this before distortion, the effect is easier to hear and control when used after.

Ambience: Finally, add delay and reverb effects for the most natural sound.

Compressors

These pedals are cousins of the big boxes found in recording studios. The are used to reduce and control the dynamic range of your playing.

Funk guitarists use compressors to "even-out" their rhythm dynamics. Country guitarists use compression for clean-picking leads. And rock guitarists even use compressors while using distortion.

While compressors can make notes sound more even, never try to use them to cover up poor technique. You want to have great control over the attack and volume of your notes, simply using your fingers.

Distortion, Overdrive and Fuzz

Talk to any sound engineer and they'll tell you these three words, distortion, overdrive and fuzz basically mean the same thing. While the terms are often interchanged, guitarists view these as unique sonic flavors with subtle musical differences.

Fuzz: The most gentle type of gain pedal. These sounds are rich in harmonics that produce a lot of excitement without straining your ears. Very popular in 1960's rock and pop.

Overdrive: Meant to simulate the overdriven circuits of guitar amplifiers. Gutsy and authoritative. Overdrive pedals powered 1970's rock.

Distortion: The most "harsh" or extreme of gain pedals. Distortion pedals range in sound from creamy and smooth to rough and raspy, or even total sonic destruction with a tight bottom for heavy metal.

Modulation

Chorus is an interesting effect that adds a kind of liquidy, spacious sound to your tone. It was invented to mimic the sound of a choir. Think about the difference in sound between one person singing, and 50 people singing. The slight differences in pitch between each voice make the choir sound easily identifyable.

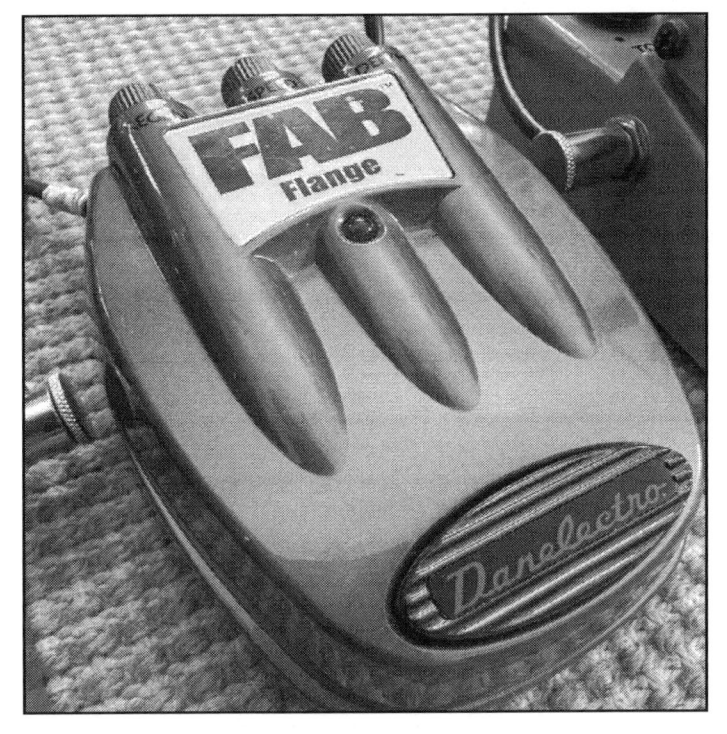

Rate and Depth: Play with the rate (speed) and depth (intensity) controls to hear how it thicken your sound.

Context Matters: Chorus works well for clean arpeggios and slow melodies.

Flangers and Phasers: These are similar effects to chorus, but with a more pronounced effect. They can produce some very funky or swirling effects.

Wah-Wah Pedals

Expression Tool: Use the wah pedal to add expression to solos and riffs. The wah-wah was invented (and named pretty well, too) to mimic the sound of a person's voice. Try one and see if you hear your guitar say, "Wah, wah!"

Experiment With Your Chain: Generally, you'll want to place the wah pedal near the end of your chain for a pronounced effect. However, guitarists differ on their sequence of wah and distortion. Try both arrangements to find out which you like. Wah into distortion produces a wide, relaxed vocal tone. Distortion into wah produces a tightly controled and focused sound that lends itself to high-gain soloing.

Reverbs and Delays

Reverb is an effect that mimics the natural reverb of big indoor spaces. Think about the sound reflections inside a large church, and you'll have a good idea about how reverb sounds.

Delay is an echo effect. Think of shouting into a canyon, "Hello..", and hearing the echoes, "Hello.. Hello..", each getting quieter. Delay controls include the time length of delay and the amount of **feedback**. Feedback adjusts how many times you'll hear each note repeat before fading away.

Subtlety is Key: Add a touch of reverb or delay for a sense of space. Avoid "muddy" overuse.

FIG. 56 - EFFECTS PEDALS

PRACTICE ROUTINES WITH DIFFERENT SOUNDS

Clean Tone Practice

Scales and Arpeggios: Practice these with a clean tone to ensure clarity.

Chord Progressions: Use a clean setting to practice rhythm and hear the nuances of different chord voicings.

Distorted Tone Practice

Riff Work: Practice your riffs with distortion to get a feel for how they will sound in a band setting.

Controlled Noise: Learn to control unwanted noise and feedback. Usually, you'll want to reduce or eliminate noise. And sometimes, you may want to really bring out the noise, bringing controlled chaos to your music!

Electric Guitar for Left-Handed Adults

46 Electric Guitar for Left-Handed Adults - Book 1 - Seeing Music Method Books

Big Open Chords: E Major and A Major

ANOTHER PAIR OF COMMON CHORDS IS THE DYNAMIC DUO OF E MAJOR AND A MAJOR. THESE CHORDS NOT ONLY RESONATE BEAUTIFULLY BUT ARE BUILDING BLOCKS FOR MANY POPULAR SONGS.

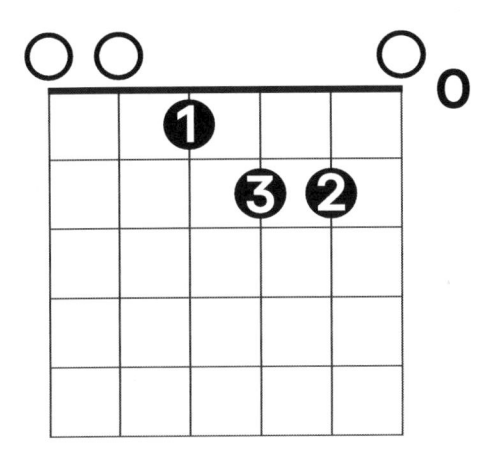

Fig.57 - E Major - Full

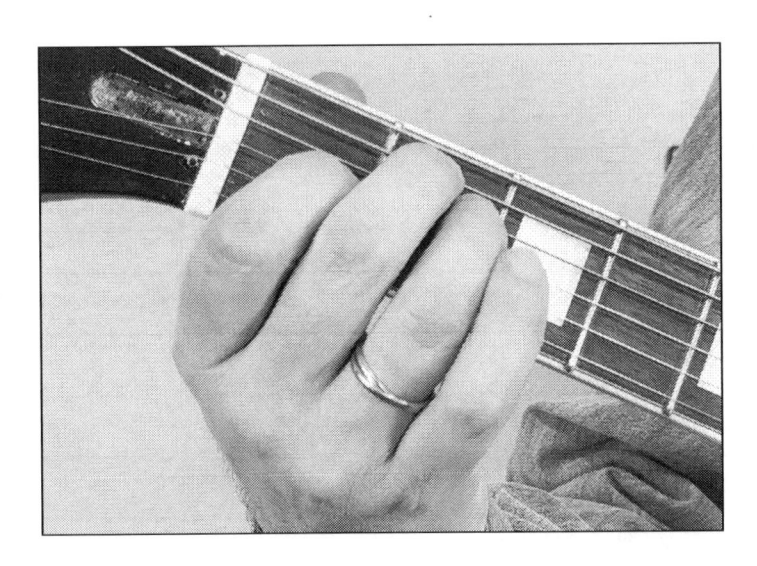

Fig.58 - E Major - Full - Hand Position

HOW TO PLAY E MAJOR

1 Start with the 6th string - it's played open, which means no fret fingers are needed.

2 Next, on the 5th string, position your 2nd finger on the 2nd fret.

3 Now on the 4th string at the 2nd fret, add your 3rd finger.

4 On the 3rd string at the 1st fret, add your 1st finger.

5 Now, maintain an arch in your hand to ensure the 2nd and 1st strings remain untouched, allowing them to ring out clearly when strummed.

6 Now, confidently strum all six strings. Ensure each note resonates clearly. If you encounter muffled notes or buzzing strings, adjust your hand positioning slightly and ensure your fingertips are close to the frets.

E AND A MAJOR 47

E MAJOR - EASY VERSION

Here's a pretty little chord and a super-easy way to play E Major.

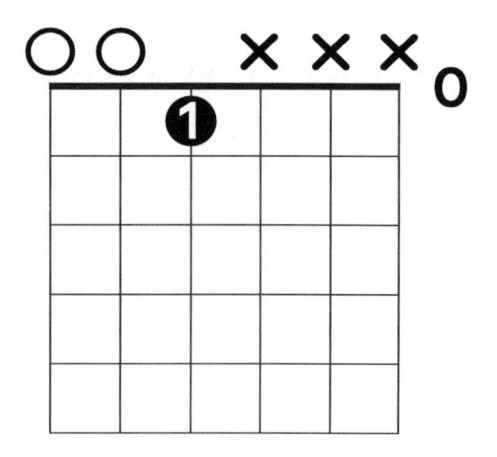

Fig.59 - E Major - Easy

1 On the 3rd string at the 1st fret, place your 1st finger.

2 Strum from the 3rd string through the 1st. Avoid hitting the 4th, 5th or 6th strings.

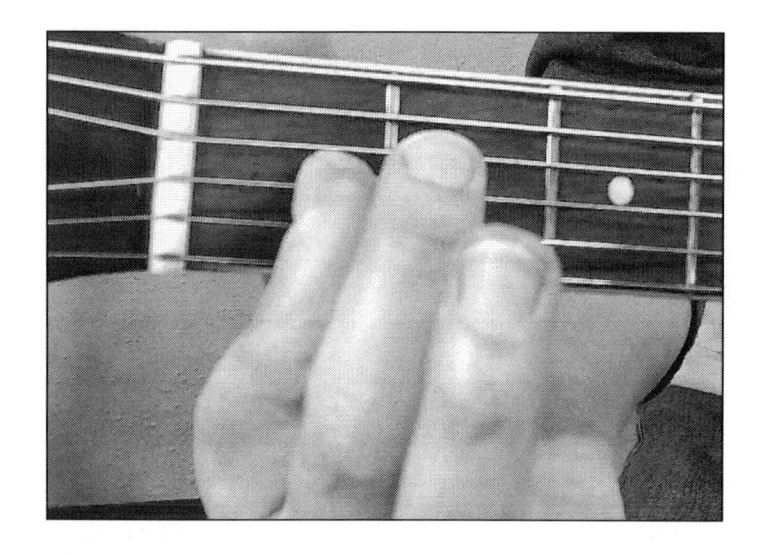

Fig.60 - E Major - Easy Hand Position

Electric Guitar for Left-Handed Adults

48 Electric Guitar for Left-Handed Adults - Book 1 - Seeing Music Method Books

HOW TO PLAY A MAJOR

1 Notice that the 6th string isn't used in this A Major chord. The 6th string has an "X" over it. So, begin with the 5th string played open. This is the open A-string.

2 On the 4th string at the 2nd fret, place your 1st finger.

3 While holding that note, you're going to add two more fingers to the next strings, all on the same fret, the 2nd fret. Add your 2nd finger to the 3rd string and your 3rd finger to the 2nd string.

4 Ensure your hand has a slight arch, letting the 1st string sound freely. The arch gets your fingers around the neck, around the fretboard and over the 1st string which you shouldn't touch.

5 Strum the first five strings, checking for clarity in each note. Adjust your positioning if necessary until each note sounds distinct.

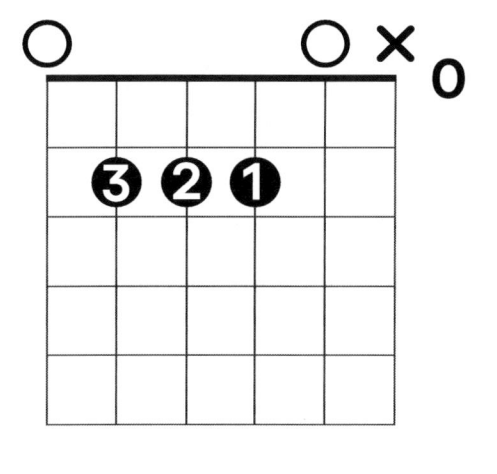

FIG.61 - A MAJOR - FULL

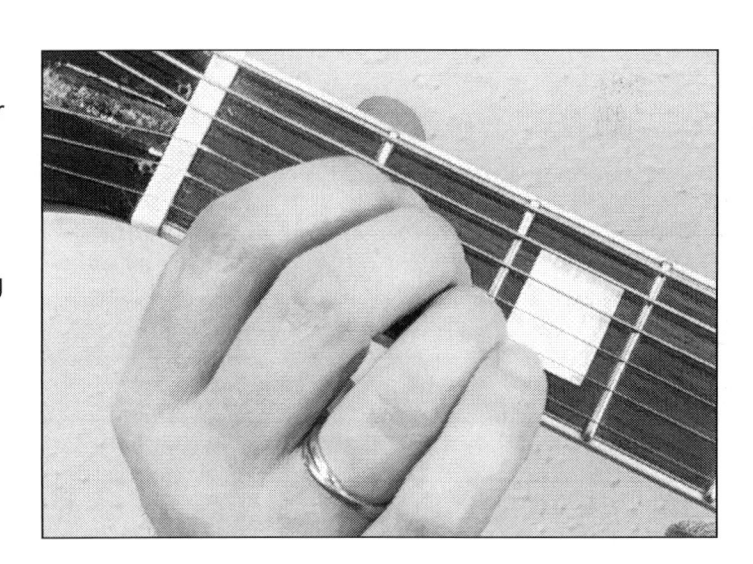

FIG.62 - A MAJOR - FULL - HAND POSITION

John Mayer: Electric Stylist

John Mayer may be known for his bluesy electric guitar solos, but his mastery extends beyond flashy riffs. His clean, soulful playing on electric guitar showcases his ability to blend genres, from blues to pop to rock, highlighting the instrument's versatility.

E AND A MAJOR 49

A MAJOR - EASY VERSION

1 On the 3rd string at the 2nd fret, place your 2nd finger. Remember to keep it close to the 2nd fret.

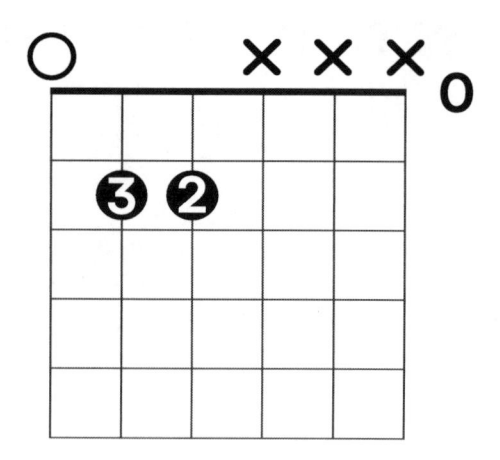

Fig.63 - A Major - Easy

2 Keeping that finger there, add the 3rd string at the 2nd fret, using your 3rd finger.

3 With your pick or thumb, strum just the 3rd, 2nd and 1st strings.

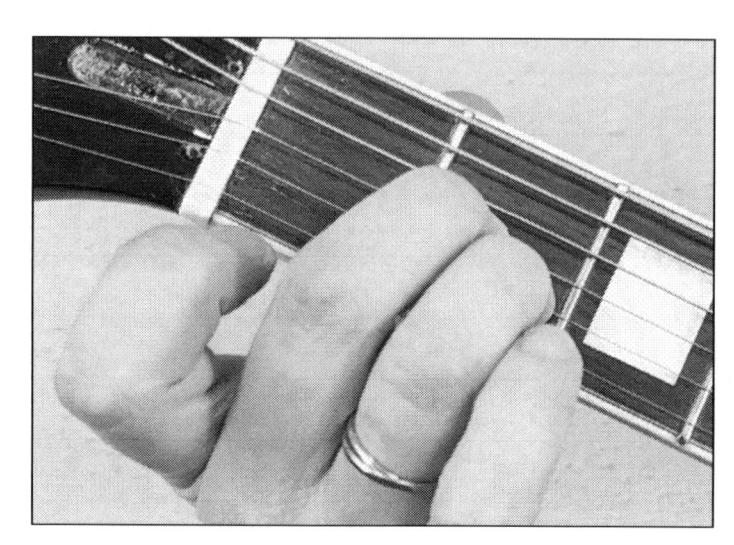

Fig.64 - A Major - Easy - Hand Position

YOU'VE BEEN INTRODUCED TO QUARTER-NOTES PREVIOUSLY. NOW EXPLORE SOME RHYTHMS THAT MERGE QUARTER-NOTES WITH HALF-NOTES.

RHYTHMIC EXERCISES

A half-note is equivalent to the duration of two quarter-notes. Count aloud: "One, Two, Three, Four". Here, each word signifies a quarter-note, while a half-note would span two counts, like "One, Two" or "Three, Four".

Try out these rhythmic patterns using the chords shown.

Listening to your progress, you're undoubtedly crafting melodies. A round of applause is in order: you're not just playing notes; you're making music! Celebrate your achievements, musician!

50 ELECTRIC GUITAR FOR LEFT-HANDED ADULTS - BOOK 1 - SEEING MUSIC METHOD BOOKS

A　C　D　E

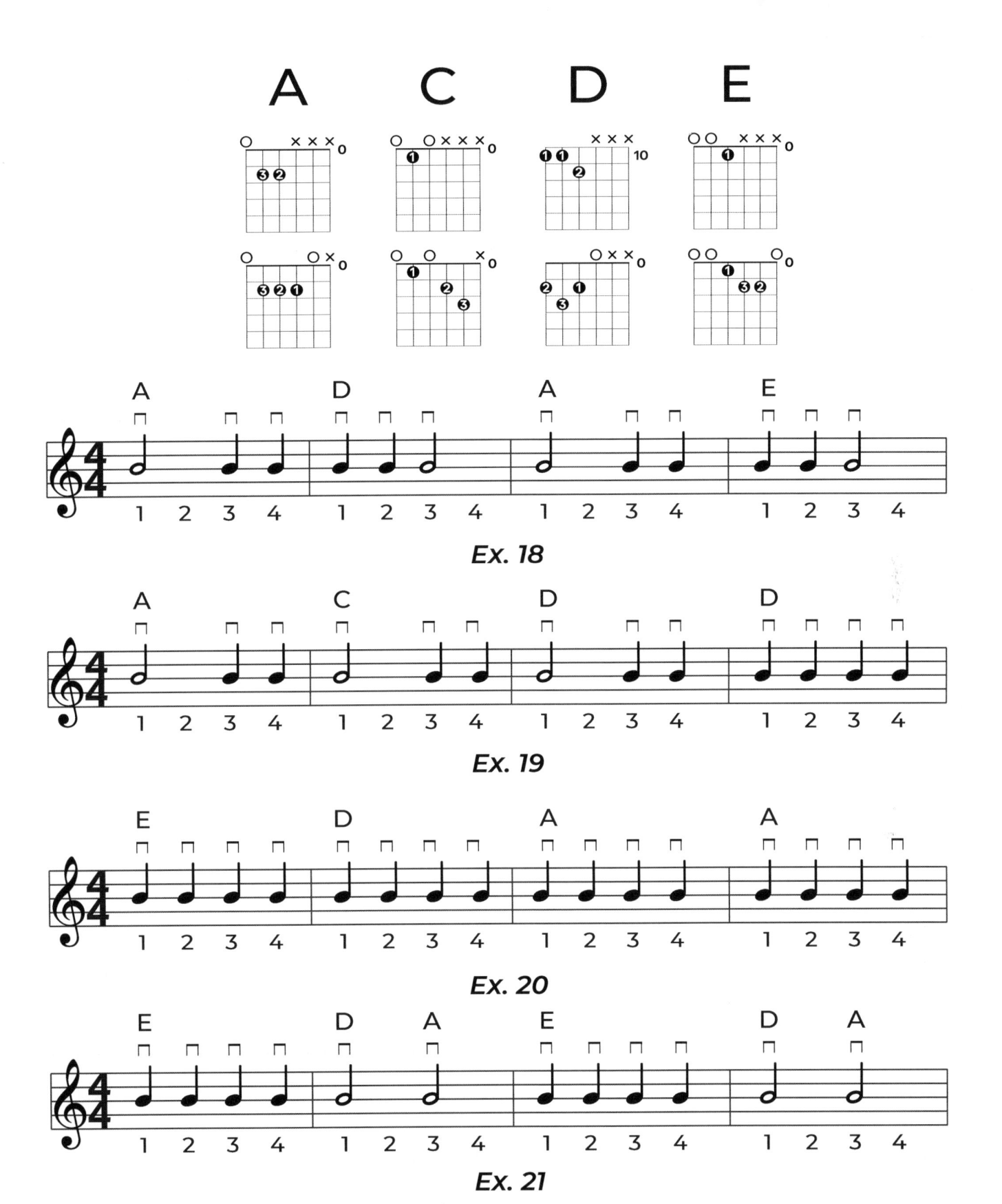

Ex. 18

Ex. 19

Ex. 20

Ex. 21

E AND A MAJOR 51

A D E

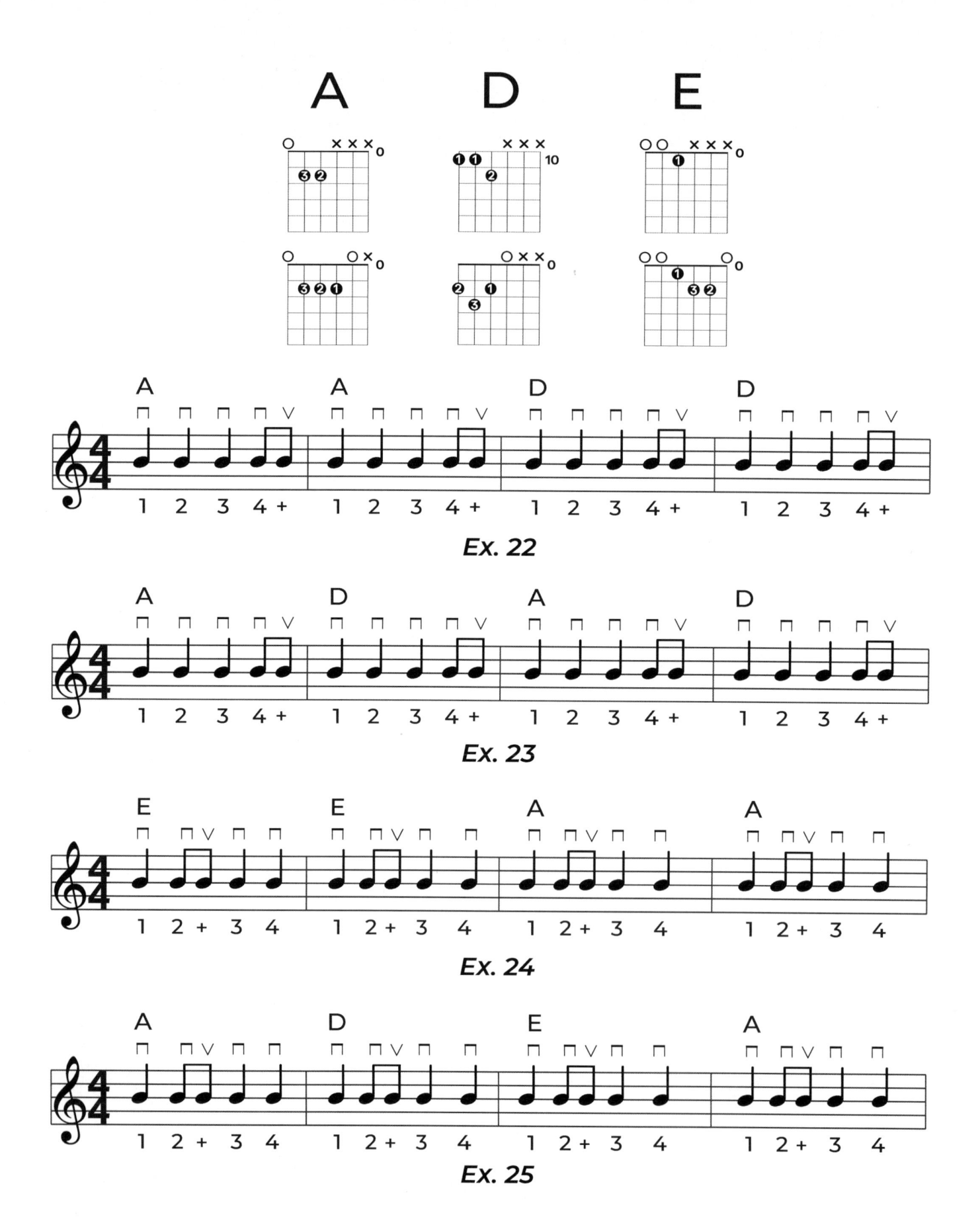

Ex. 22

Ex. 23

Ex. 24

Ex. 25

52 Electric Guitar for Left-Handed Adults - Book 1 - Seeing Music Method Books

Learn Minor Chords: E and A Minor

EVERY MAJOR CHORD HAS ITS MINOR VERSION, TOO. NOW THAT YOU'VE PLAYED E AND A MAJOR, YOU'LL REALLY ENJOY LEARNING THEIR MINOR COUNTERPARTS.

HOW TO PLAY E MINOR

Fig.65 - E Minor - Full

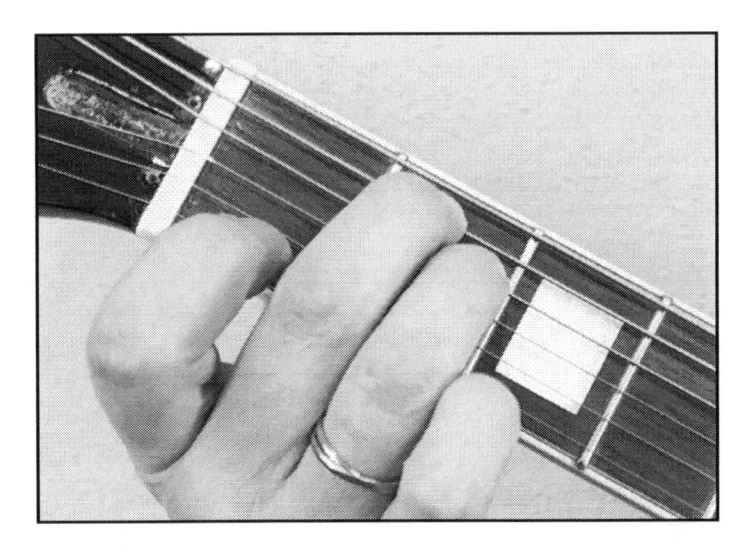

Fig.66 - E Minor - Full Hand Position

1 You're going to recognize many of these notes from E Major. Start with the open-6th string. Play it without a fretting finger.

2 Next, on the 5th string at the 2nd fret, position your 2nd finger.

3 At the 4th string, 2nd fret, add your 3rd finger.

4 Maintain an arch in your hand to ensure the 3rd, 2nd and 1st strings remain untouched, allowing them to ring out clearly when strummed.

5 Now, give a strum to all six strings and hear the big, rich sound.

The Versatility of E Minor

Big and beautiful, E Minor is a versatile chord, fitting seamlessly into genres ranging from classical to heavy metal.

Minor chords tend to sound sad, where Major sounds happy.

E AND A MINOR 53

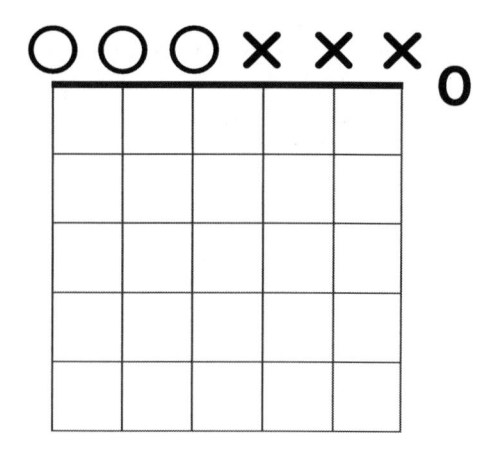

Fig. 67 - E Minor - Easy

E MINOR - EASY VERSION

How about a chord that doesn't require any fingers? Sounds good!

1 Strum from the 3rd string through the 1st, just those three strings. Just one step: That's it!

HOW TO PLAY A MINOR

1 Just like A Major, the 6th string isn't involved in the A Minor chord. The 6th string has an "X" over it. So, begin with the 5th string played open.

2 On the 4th string at the 2nd fret, place your 2nd finger.

3 While holding that note, on the 3rd string at the 2nd fret add your 3rd finger and on the 2nd string at the 1st fret, add your 1st finger.

4 Ensure your hand has a slight arch, letting the 1st string sound freely.

5 Give your A Minor chord a strum. Does each note sound approximately the same volume? Did you remember to not hit the 6th string?

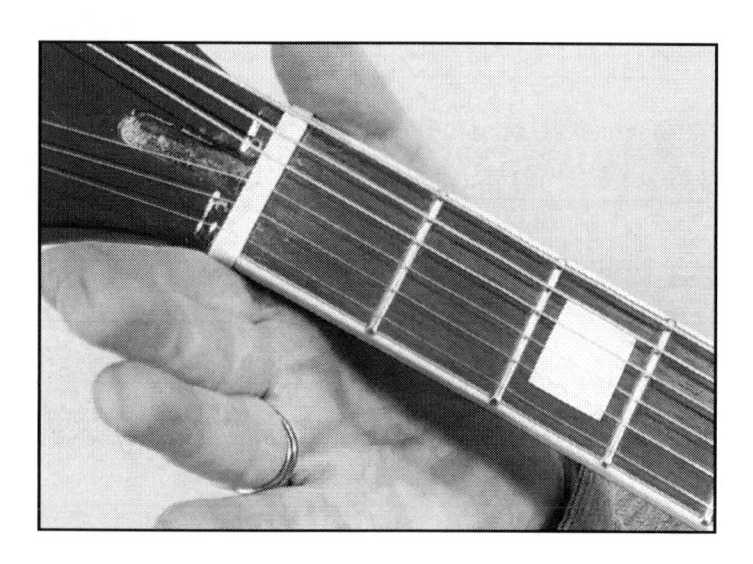

Fig. 68 - E Minor - Easy Hand Position

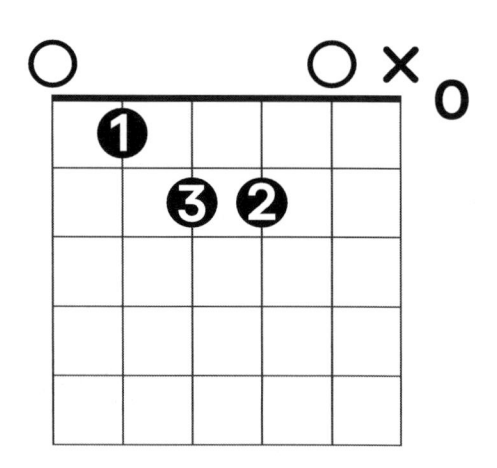

Fig. 69 - A Minor - Full

Fig. 70 - A Minor - Full Hand Position

54 ELECTRIC GUITAR FOR LEFT-HANDED ADULTS - BOOK 1 - SEEING MUSIC METHOD BOOKS

A MINOR - EASY VERSION

1 On the 3rd string at the 2nd fret, place your 2nd finger. Remember to keep it close to the 2nd fret.

2 Keeping that finger there, add the 2nd string at the 1st fret, using your 1st finger.

3 With your pick or thumb, strum just the 3rd through 1st strings.

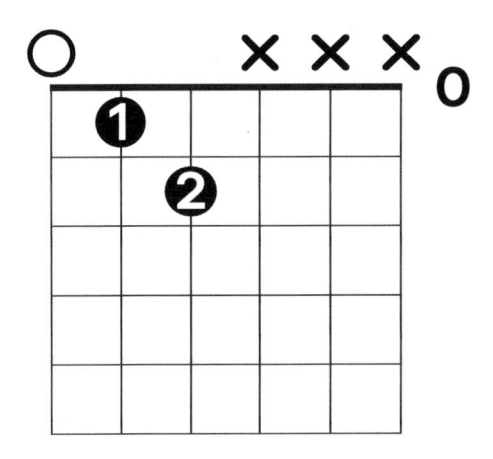

Fig.71 - A Minor - Easy

A Minor's Melancholic Beauty

A Minor is often associated with a somber and reflective mood in music, making it a go-to key for emotional songs.

Fig.72 - A Minor - Easy Hand Position

Women Guitarists Who Shaped Music

Pioneering women like Memphis Minnie and Maybelle Carter played pivotal roles in the development of blues and country guitar styles.

Today, classical guitarist Sharon Isbin is regarded as one of the very best to have ever played the instrument.

E AND A MINOR 55

EXERCISES FOR A MINOR AND E MINOR

Ex. 26

Ex. 27

Ex. 28

Ex. 29

**You've already learned a LOT of chords and rhythms.
Whenever learning new music, take the time to slow down the tempo.
Slowing down makes it easier to play correctly. Speed will come later.**

A min C D E min G

Ex. 30

Ex. 31

Ex. 32

Ex. 33

E AND A MINOR 57

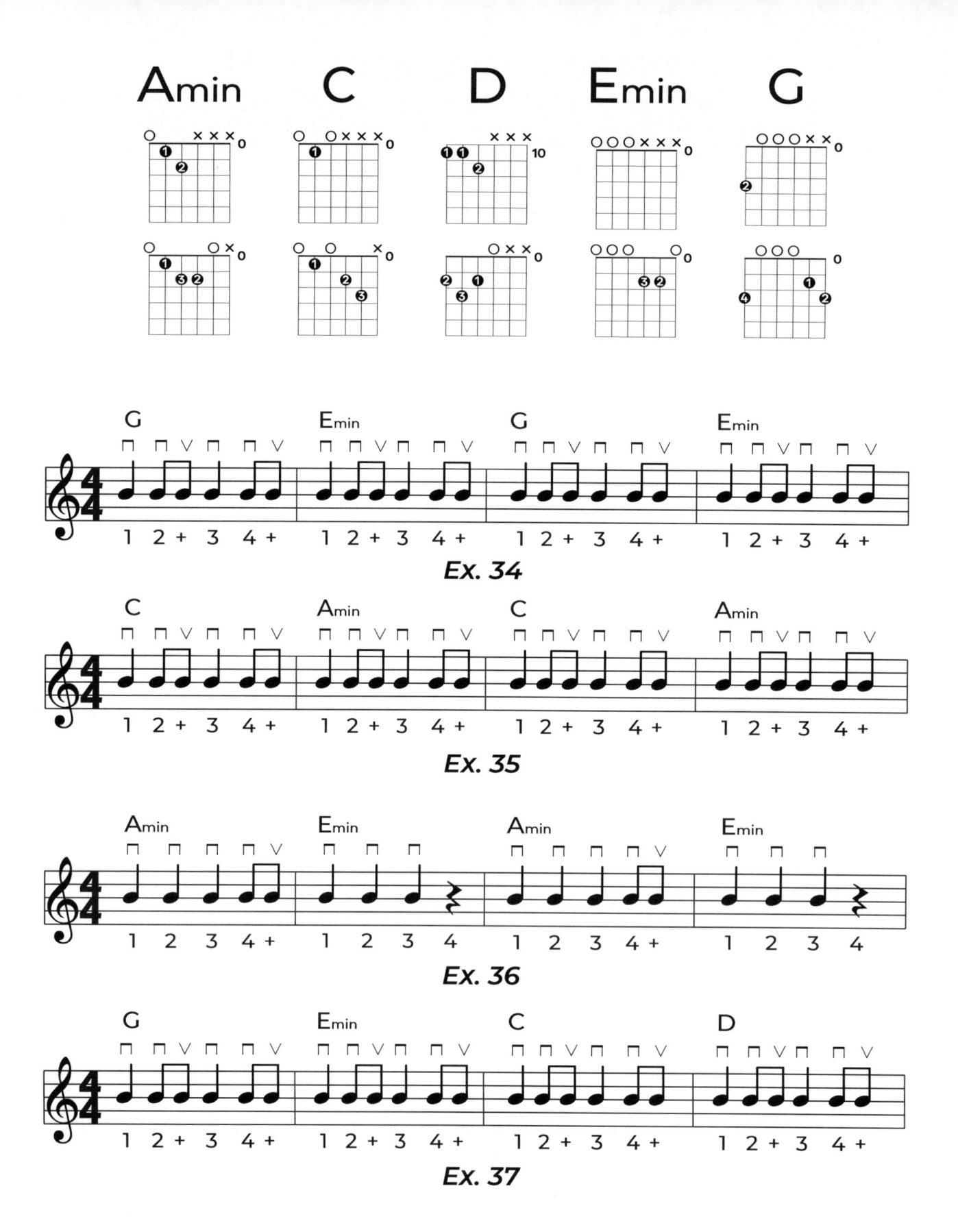

58 ELECTRIC GUITAR for LEFT-HANDED ADULTS - BOOK 1 - SEEING MUSIC METHOD BOOKS

Rhythm Guitar Gold - Power Chords, Octaves and Chord Fragments

GREAT GUITARISTS HAVE MANY WAYS TO PLAY A CHORD: SOME COMPLEX, SOME VERY EASY BUT STILL GREAT SOUNDING. SO FAR, YOU'VE LEARNED ENTIRE CHORDS, SOME USING 5 AND 6 NOTES AT ONCE. NOW TRY THESE SIMPLE VARIATIONS THAT ARE FUN AND FANTASTIC.

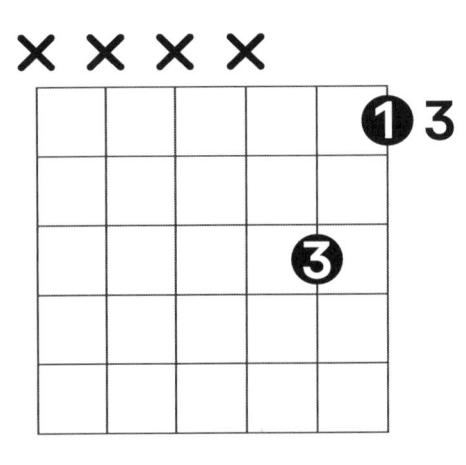

FIG.124 - G5 POWER CHORD

INTRODUCTION TO POWER CHORDS

it's time to introduce a type of chord that adds raw energy and punch to your playing - the **power chord**. Power chords are the backbone of rock, punk, and metal music. Despite their simplicity, they bring a solid and powerful sound to your guitar playing.

What is a Power Chord?

A power chord, technically known as a "fifth chord," is made up of only two different notes: the root and the fifth. Unlike major or minor chords, power chords are neither - they are neutral. This lack of musical "color" makes them incredibly versatile and a favorite for electric guitarists, especially when distortion is applied.

PLAY YOUR FIRST POWER CHORD

The Basic Shape

1 Start with the Root: Place your index finger on the 3rd fret of the 6th string. This is the note G, which is the root.

2 Add the Fifth: Place your ring finger on the 5th fret of the 5th string. This is the note D, the fifth of the chord.

3 Strum only the two strings you are pressing.

You've just played a G5 power chord! The simplicity of its form allows for quick movements across the fretboard, which is useful in fast-paced musical styles.

> Great rhythm guitarists know how to use lots of different chord voicings, both simple and complex, to fill out their guitar parts.

SIMPLE RHYTHM CHORDS 59

WHY PLAY POWER CHORDS?

Clarity in Distortion

Try playing a G major chord with heavy distortion, and then play a G5 power chord. Notice how much clearer the power chord sounds. This clarity, even in high distortion settings, is why power chords are prevalent in rock and metal genres.

FIG.125 - G Major Chord

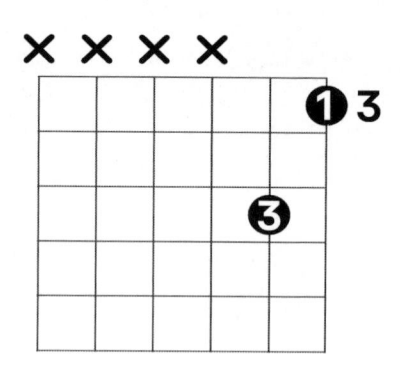

FIG.126 - G5 Power Chord

Moving Power Chords Up and Down the Neck

Power chords are "movable" chords, meaning the shape doesn't change as you move up and down the neck. Much like barre chords, this is a huge help for guitarists. One power chord can become a different one, simply by moving it to a new starting fret location. Both chords use the same chord **shape**. This lets you quickly change chords without having to adjust your fingers too much.

Check out these power chords, below.

1 Start with the same G5 chord you played before. Remember that the root is G, played by your 1st finger on the 6th string.

2 Move both fingers up the neck two frets. This is an A5. The root note has moved from G to A. A is at the 5th fret on the 6th string.

3 Again, move both fingers up the neck another two frets. This is a B5. The root note has moved from A to B. B is at the 7th fret on the 6th string.

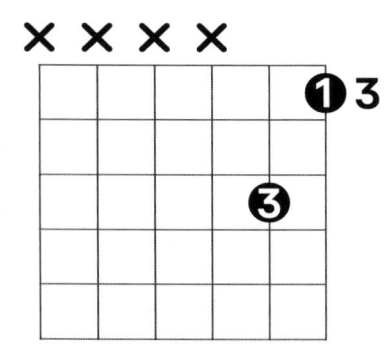

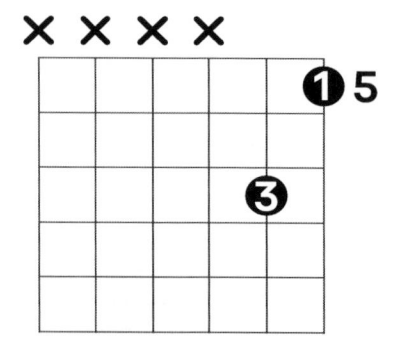

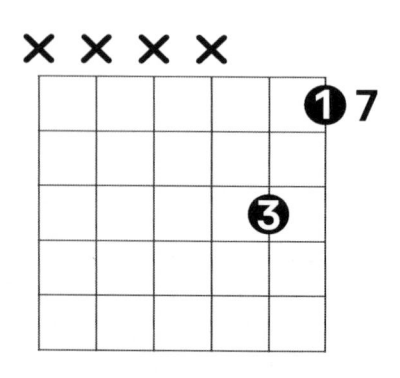

FIG.127 - G5 Power Chord

FIG.128 - A5 Power Chord

FIG.129 - B5 Power Chord

Moving Power Chords Across the Neck

Power chords generally have their root on the 6th or 5th string. These are considered the bass strings of the guitar and that low-end energy puts the **power** in a power chord.

Check out these power chords, below.

1 Start with a 5th-String Root: Place your 1st finger on the 3rd fret of the 5th string. This is the note C, which is the root.

2 Add the Fifth: Place your ring finger on the 5th fret of the 4th string. This is the note G, the *fifth* of the chord.

3 Strum only the two strings you are pressing.

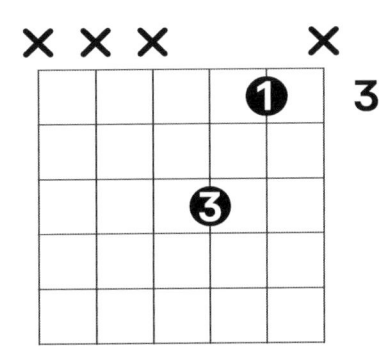

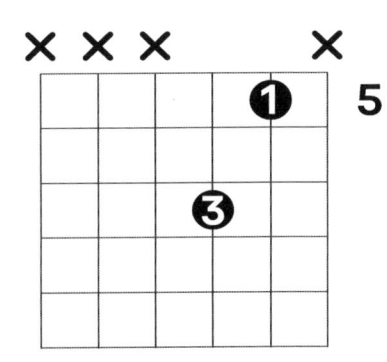

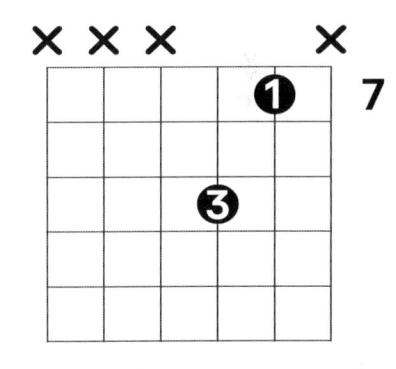

Fig.130 - C5 Power Chord

Fig.131 - D5 Power Chord

Fig.132 - E5 Power Chord

When to Use Power Chords

Enhancing Rhythms: Power chords have a natural rhythmic emphasis.

Rhythmic Foundation: Use power chords to play the main riff of a rock song.

Dynamics: Play around with the intensity of your strumming to feel the difference in dynamics and energy.

SIMPLE RHYTHM CHORDS

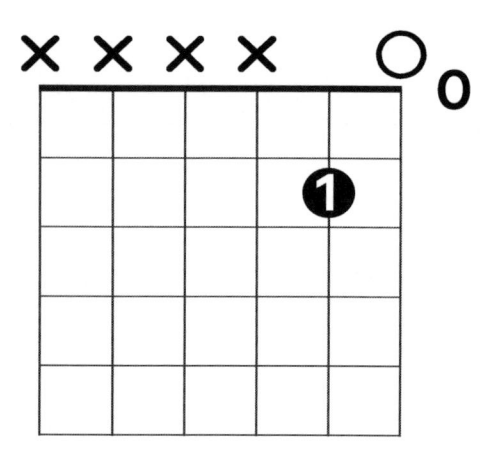

Fig.133 - E5 Power Chord

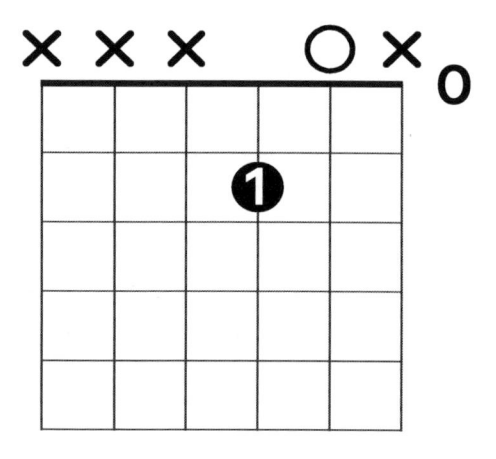

Fig.134 - A5 Power Chord

E5 and A5

This is where Rock lives! E5 and A5 are probably the two most important chords to Rock guitarists. They both use an open string which just sounds huge. Get ready to rock!

1 Play E5: Place your 1st finger on the 2nd fret of the 5th string. Play just the 6th and 5th strings, muting the others with your fretting hand.

2 Play A5: Move your 1st finger to the 2nd fret of the 4th string.

BE A POWER CHORD POWERHOUSE

Palm Muting and Slides

Palm Muting: Rest the edge of your palm lightly on the strings near the bridge and strum. This gives a chunky, muted sound that's iconic in rock music.

Slides: Slide the power chord shape up and down the neck without lifting your fingers to create a smooth transition between chords.

Tips for Clean Power Chords

- Muting Unused Strings: Use the edge of your fretting hand to lightly touch and mute the adjacent strings that you're not playing.

- Hand Strength: Power chords can be tiring. Regular practice will help build the necessary hand strength and endurance.

Practice Makes Power

Practice transitioning between power chords using different strumming patterns and tempos. Remember, power chords are about confidence and attitude, so play them with conviction.

OCTAVES

Almost in their own category, octaves are simply two pitches with the same name, one *octave* apart. They aren't exactly chords, but they are a nice way to embellish your part while adding a familiar sound. Think of them as big, fat versions of single notes. A single note plus it's octave note will sound almost as full as a power chord, and they're really fun to play.

In concept, octaves are the way musical scales and notes repeat themselves across our range of hearing. The piano has 8 octaves and you can see the pattern of black and white keys repeating 8 times across any piano. The notes repeat their sequence in each octave.

> Use these octaves now! Have a look at the song "Jeanie Blue Eyes" near the end of this book. The rhythm guitar uses octaves to create the guitar part.

Play Some Octaves

Try each octave below, listening for their big, ringing sounds.

1 Begin by placing your 1st finger on the 5th string at the fret indicated in the upper corner.

2 Add your 4th finger to the 3rd string. You can think of this as "two strings over, and two frets up".

3 Notice how the 4th string is not played? You'll need to mute that string with the side of your 1st finger. Dampen the string slightly while you're still pressing down on the fretted 5th string.

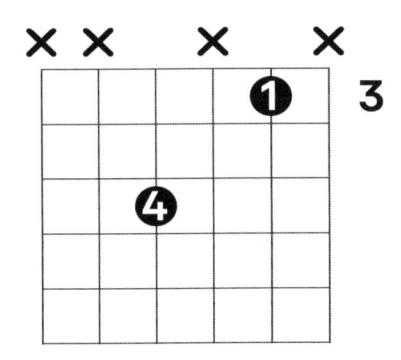

FIG.135 - C OCTAVE

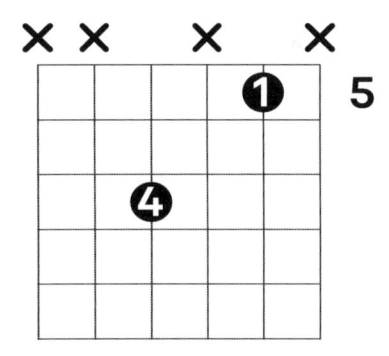

FIG.136 - D OCTAVE

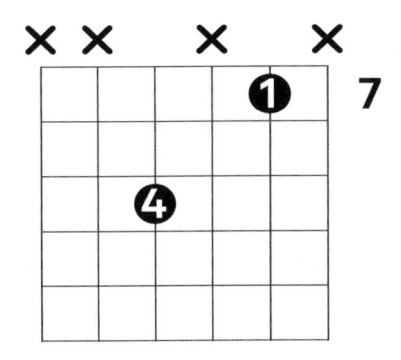

FIG.137 - E OCTAVE

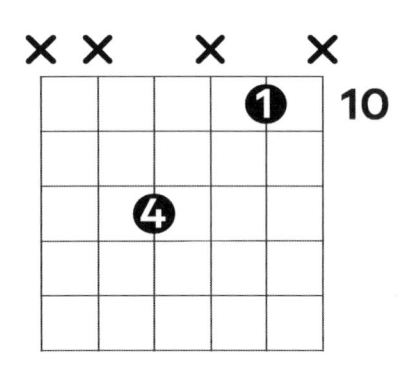

FIG.138 - G OCTAVE

SIMPLE RHYTHM CHORDS

RHYTHM CHORDS

Guitarists are great at recycling. Just like recycling metal and plastic gives those items a new life, re-using chords in new and creative ways is the best way to make your music much more interesting.

Now, you already know lots of full chords. Here, you'll learn how to select small pieces of those chords to create tight little rhythm chords that sound great with a full band. There's nothing new to memorize here. You'll just be selecting a few notes from bigger chords you've already learned. This method works in virtually every song and is easy to master.

Chop It Up

As the electric guitarist in a band, at any time you have the option to either play the full chord or just a part of it. When there's not a lot of other people playing in the same register (like keyboards, guitars and background vocals, etc.), then full chords sound full and great.

However, when several instruments are playing, it may be better to just play a small part of a chord. It's not necessary to play every note all the time. And, small chords sound great amplified - often giving a cleaned up and punchy rhythm.

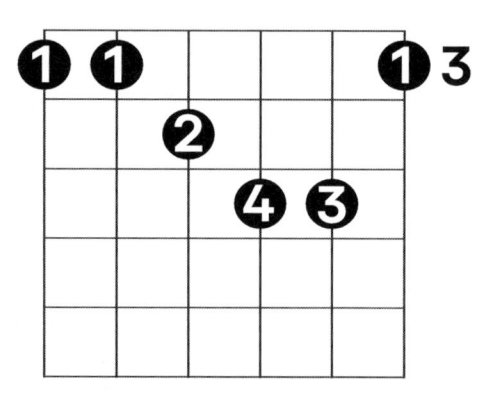

Fig.139 - G Major Barre Chord

1 Consider a G Major barre chord. It has 6 notes and sounds really big and full. Play all 6 notes now and listen to the big sound. Keep your fingers there.

2 Now one-at-a-time, play each of the chord fragments. Only play the black notes. The grey show where your fingers should still be resting. These are small pieces of the whole chord you just played. Your right hand doesn't have to move, just vary your picking to strike only the strings shown with black dots. Can you hear the sound change from low-register notes, to middle, to high?

Low Strings   **Middle Strings**   **High Strings**

Fig.140 - Low Notes   *Fig.141 - Middle Notes*   *Fig.142 - High Notes*

64 Electric Guitar for Left-Handed Adults - Book 1 - Seeing Music Method Books

Do those three chord fragments sound good together?
You bet they do!

Any time you need to play a chord, you now have four choices for how to play it: Full, low-register, middle-register or upper-register.

> **Play Small Rhythm Chords**
>
> Hear this technique used on the song, "Midnight Mirage" and "Disco, Ball".

Arpeggios

What a fancy word! An arpeggio is a chord played one note-at-a-time. As opposed to strumming, where all the strings are played at once with a rapidly moving pick hand, arpeggios single out each note. These are a great way to add drama or suspense to your guitar line.

Arpeggios can be beautiful and really useful anywhere around the neck, high or low. Just listen to this arpeggio made up of notes on the middle strings.

See the full chord at right? You'll recognize the G Major barre chord. Instead of playing all the notes this time, you'll place your fingers for just the black dot notes using the fingers shown. Get ready to play the arpeggio by first placing your three fingers, then playing the note one-at-a-time as indicated below.

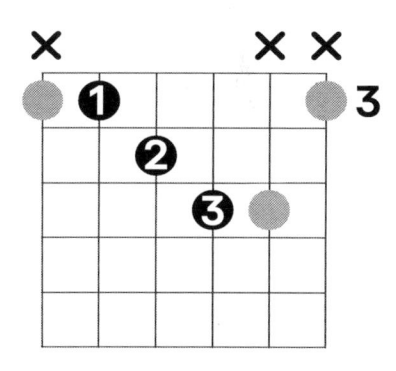

FIG.143 - G MAJOR BARRE CHORD

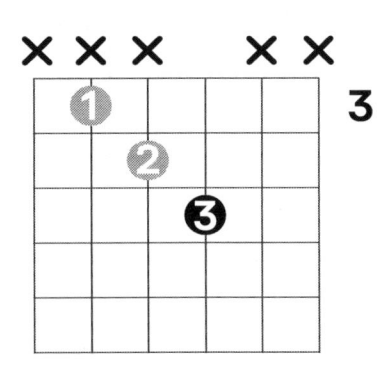

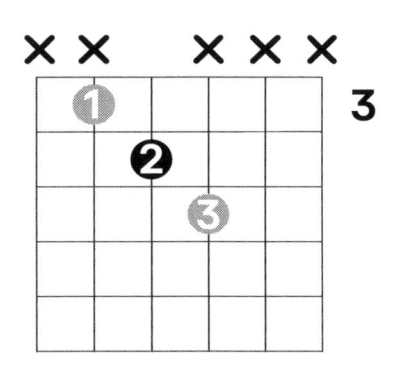

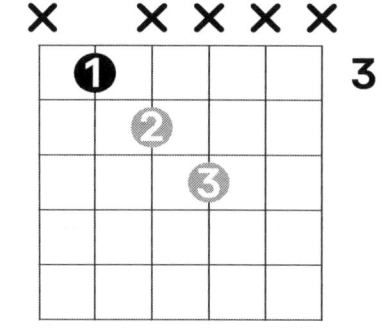

FIG.144 - G MAJOR ARPEGGIO

> Hear this technique used on the songs, "Bird of Freedom" and "Whiskey, Wagons, Wheels".

SIMPLE RHYTHM CHORDS 65

And here is another arpeggio, made from a different group of three G Major notes. This arpeggio sounds neat on just the lowest strings.

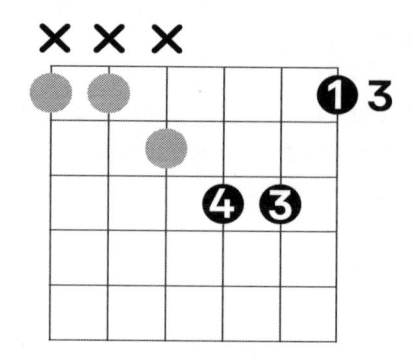

Fig.145 - G5 Chord

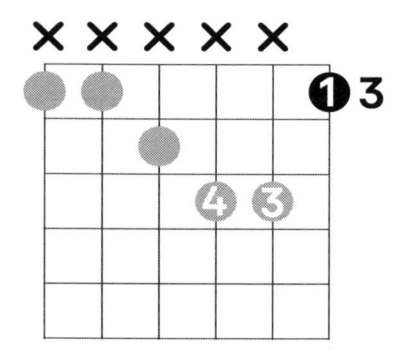

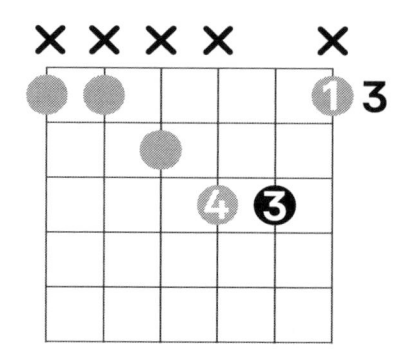

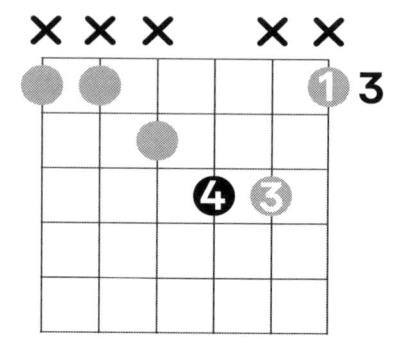

Fig.146 - G5 Arpeggio

Ready to get more from your fretboard?

Loads of great exercises to put your memory to work.

seeingmusicbooks.com

Song Workshop: Learn with Your Favorite Styles

EVERY MUSICIAN HAS A FAVORITE STYLE OR GENRE. FIND YOURS HERE AND DIG IN TO SOME RHYTHM PATTERNS YOU'LL ENJOY.

FOREVER CLASSICS

Auld Lang Syne

> This quarter rest is a "Pick-Up Note". It's the lead-in beat of the song.
>
> The vocal sings it alone, then you strum beginning at the next measure.

Verse

| 4 | 1 | 2 | 3 | 4 | continue rhythm... |
| Should | auld | a-cquan-tance | be | for- got, and... |

auld lang syne, my dear for auld lang syne,...

Chorus — For

1 2 3 4 | 1 2 3 4

SONG WORKSHOP 67

Swing Low, Sweet Chariot

Chorus

Traditional Spiritual

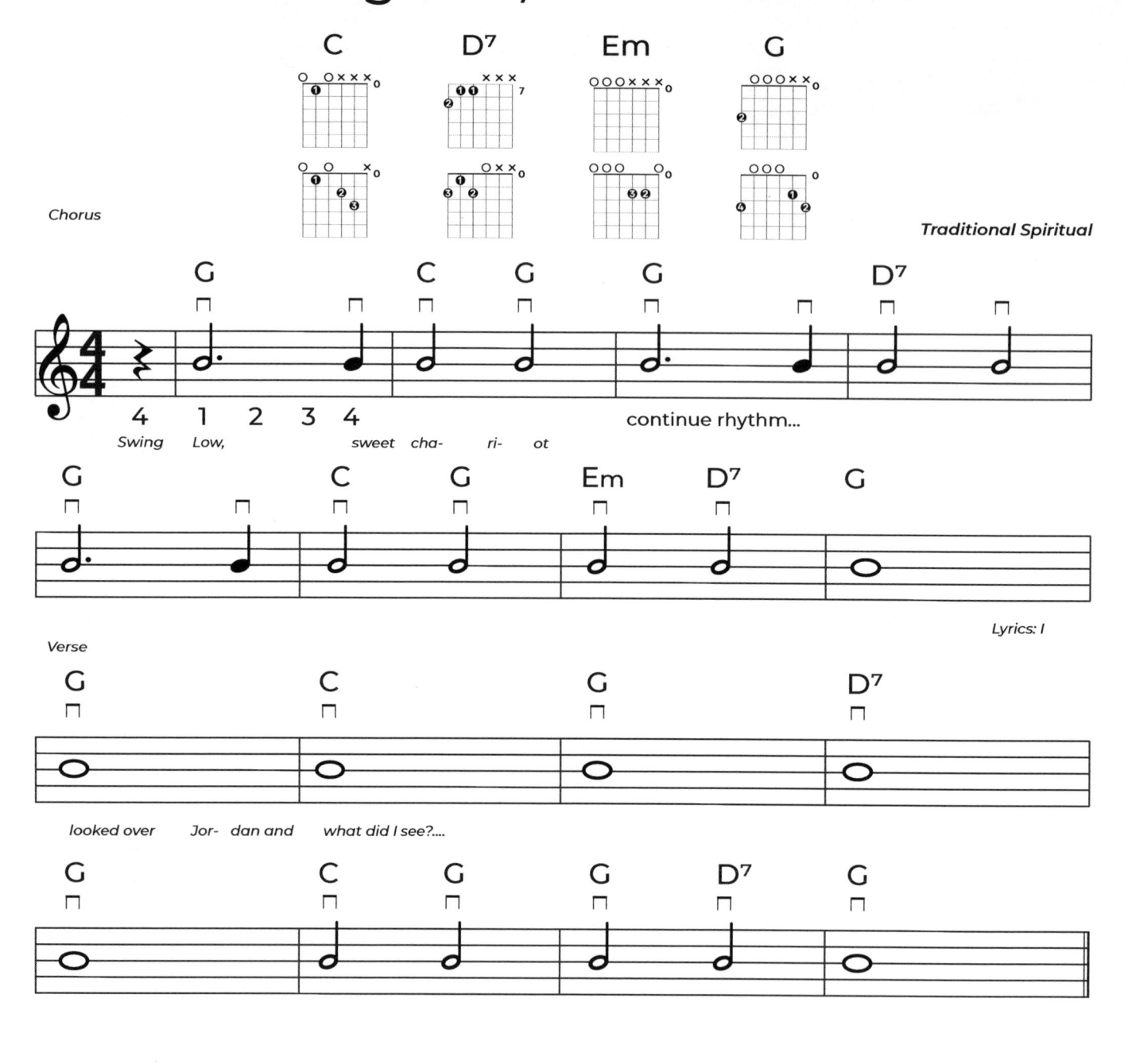

Swing Low, sweet cha- ri- ot
continue rhythm...

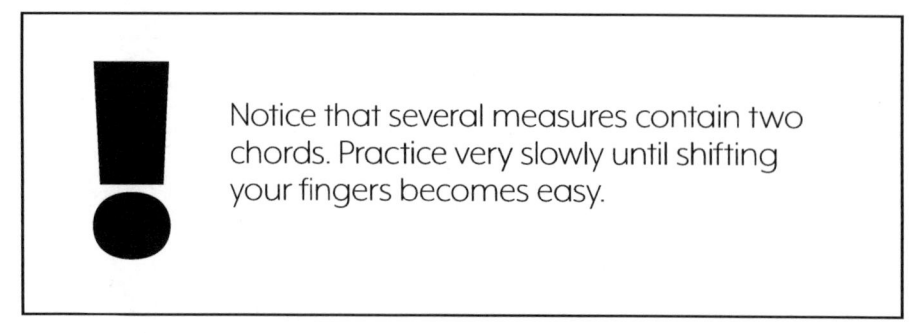

looked over Jor- dan and what did I see?....

Verse

Lyrics: I

> **!** Notice that several measures contain two chords. Practice very slowly until shifting your fingers becomes easy.

68 ELECTRIC GUITAR FOR LEFT-HANDED ADULTS - BOOK 1 - SEEING MUSIC METHOD BOOKS

50'S ROCK AND ROLL

Rock, Roll and Rumble

See how the rhythm changes in the 4th and 8th measures? In those measures, stop your strings on beat 4.

Rhythm was all-important to 1950s jukebox hits. Hit songs had a unique and memorable beat, often made for dancing.

Notice the exciting and varied rhythms in this song. Rock it up!

SONG WORKSHOP 69

80'S RADIO

Valley Life Dolls

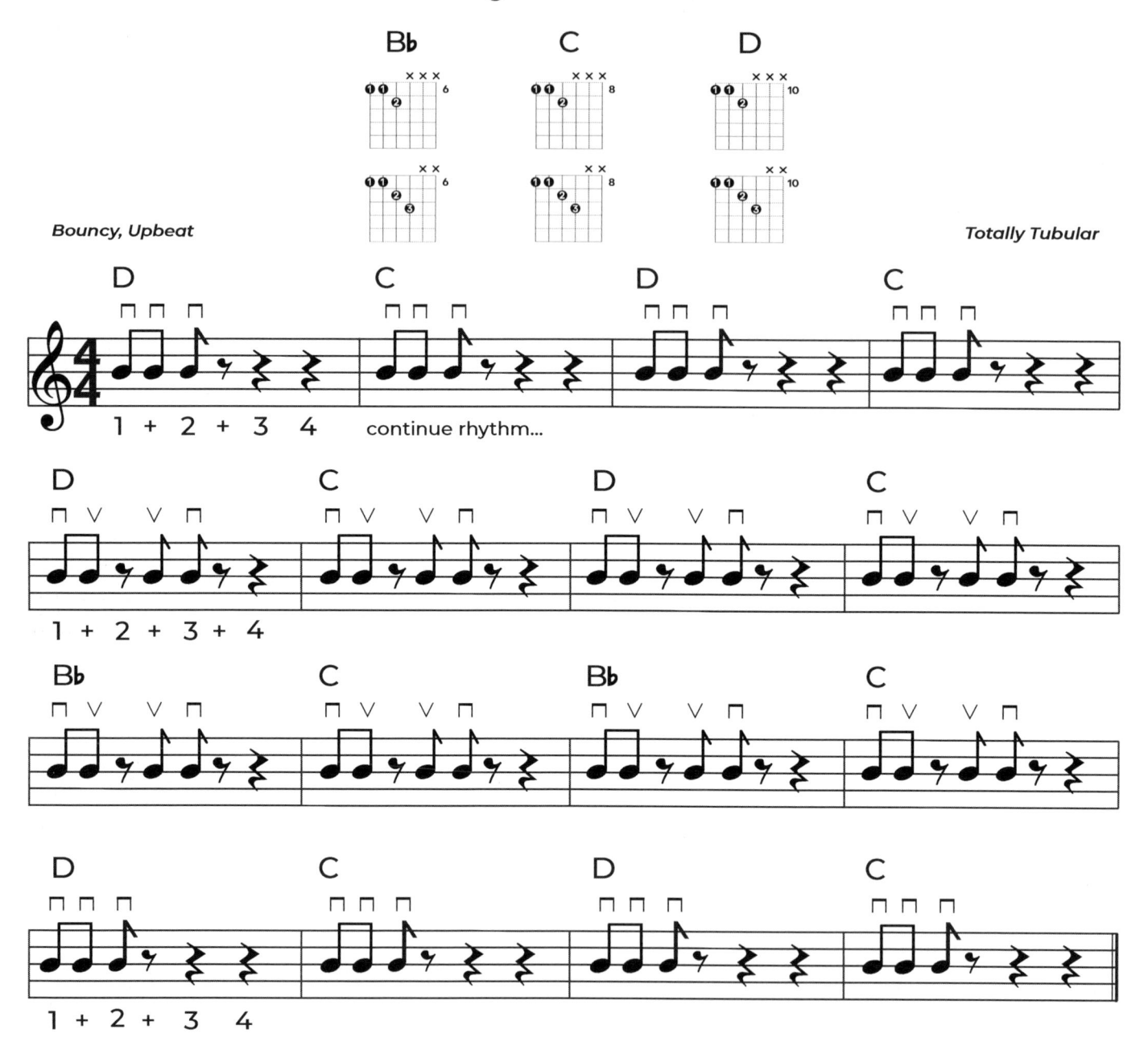

Bb   C   D

Bouncy, Upbeat　　　　　　　　　　　　　　　　　　　　　　　*Totally Tubular*

The Eighties: The Era of Big Hair and Bold Chords

The '80s are famous for soaring electric guitar solos and bold power chords, defining the decade's sound. From the anthemic riffs of rock bands to the innovative use of effects, the electric guitar was at the heart of both the era's hard-hitting tracks and emotive power ballads.

Midnight Mirage

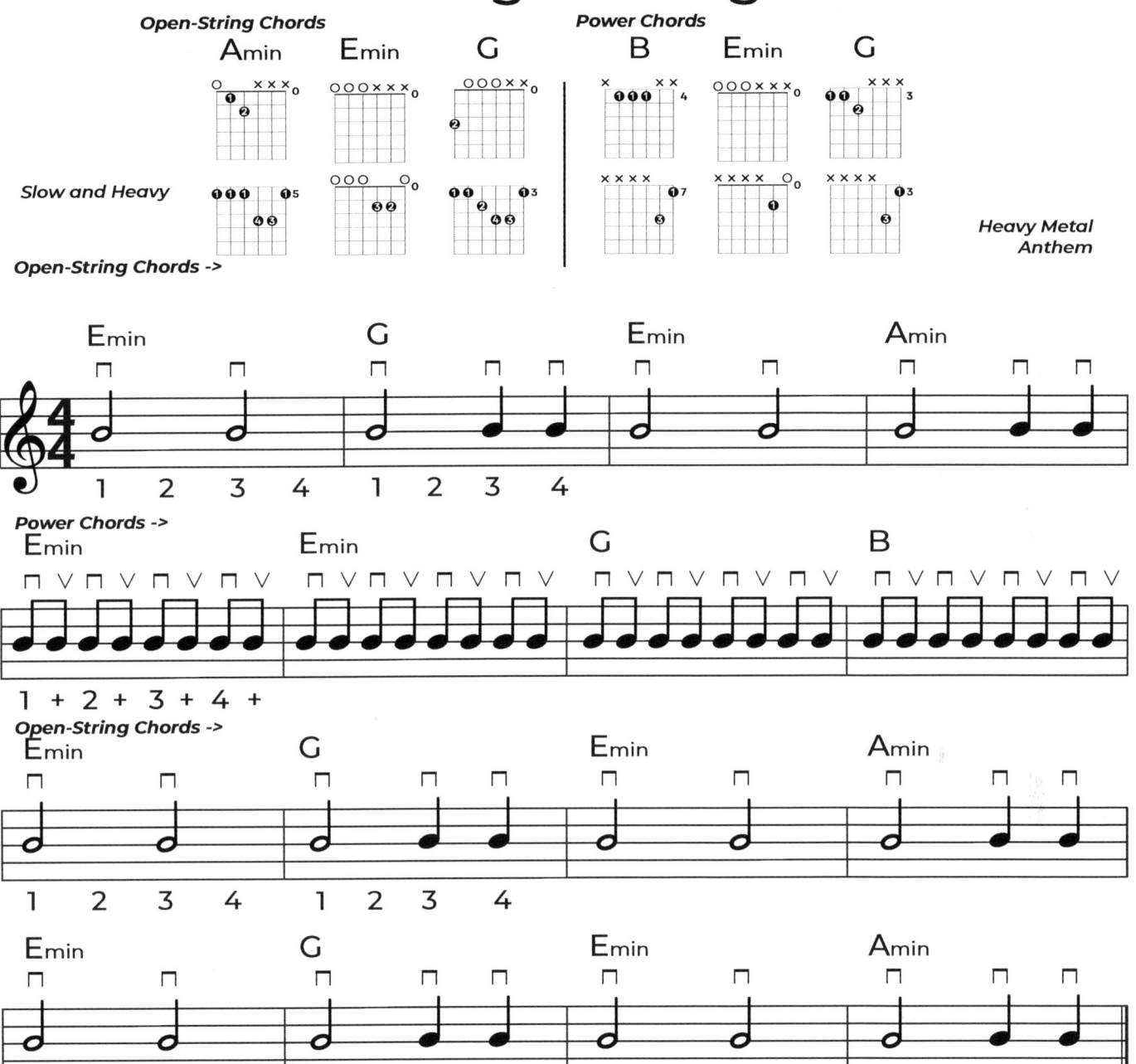

Open-String Chords **Power Chords**

Amin   Emin   G   B   Emin   G

Slow and Heavy

Open-String Chords ->

Heavy Metal Anthem

Power Chords ->

Open-String Chords ->

Power Chords

This song introduces Power Chords. Power chords strip away the higher pitched notes of the chord, leaving just the bottom notes. While not as harmonically rich as their full versions, their stripped, bassy sound has great impact and power, as the name implies.

After you learn this song with a clean sound, try a little overdrive or distortion from your amp or effects pedals for some loud Rock fun!

SONG WORKSHOP

OLD-TIME COUNTRY & AMERICANA
Whiskey, Wagons, Wheels

Bouncing *Outlaw Country*

Outlaw Country: The Renegades of Nashville

"Outlaw Country emerged in the 1970s as a rebellion against the polished Nashville sound. Led by mavericks like Willie Nelson and Waylon Jennings, these artists broke from mainstream country's constraints, producing music that was raw, honest, and reflected their rugged lifestyles. The term 'Outlaw' was coined from their nonconformity to the industry norms and their songs that often celebrated the outlaw persona.

A Cowboy on One Knee

Pensively — *Early Americana*

3/4 time

Measure 1: C — 1 2 3
Measure 2: C — continue rhythm...
Measure 3: F
Measure 4: F

Measure 5: G
Measure 6: F
Measure 7: C
Measure 8: C

Measure 9: F
Measure 10: F
Measure 11: C
Measure 12: C

Measure 13: G
Measure 14: F
Measure 15: C
Measure 16: C

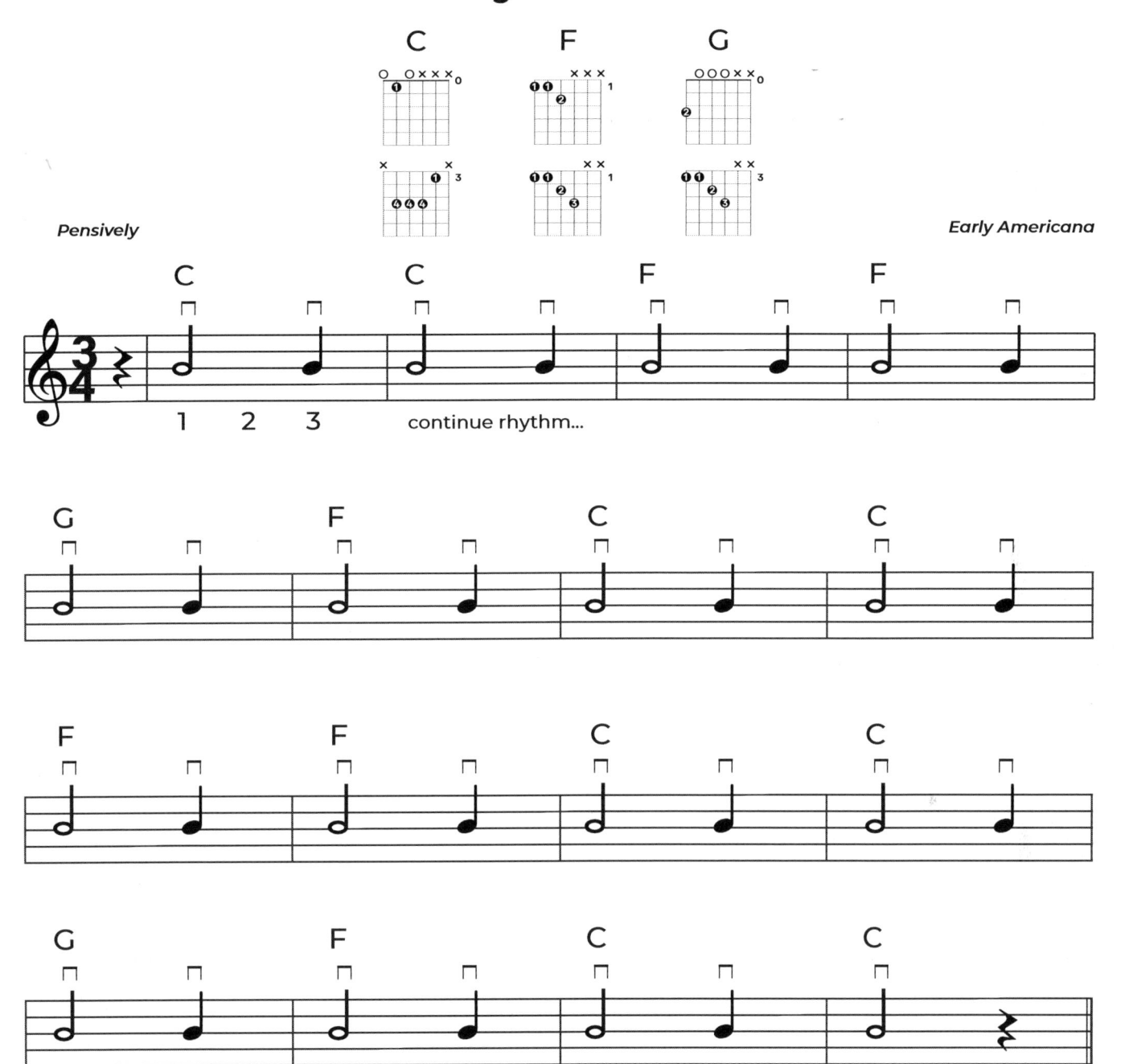

Country Music and the Electric Guitar

Buck Owens shaped country music in the 1960s with his "Bakersfield Sound," defined by the twangy tones of electric Fender Telecasters. His raw, energetic style, highlighted by lead guitarist Don Rich's clean picking and minimal effects, set him apart from the smoother Nashville sound. Owens' use of the electric guitar influenced both country and rock, leaving a lasting legacy.

SONG WORKSHOP 73

SEEING MUSIC
Many Scales and Modes
by Root and Scale Type
Fingerings for Each Scale
Spell Common and Exotic Scales
Modes, Pentatonics and More
LEFT-HANDED
ENCYCL
Fast Reference for All Playing Styles
Organized by Root, Style and Chord Type
Multiple Voicings for Many Chords
Learn Barred, Portable and Open-String Fingerings
Both Triadic and Drop Voicings Using 4ths & 5ths
Fast Reference for
You Need in
LEFT-HANDED GUITA
CHORDS
ENCYCLOPEDIA
ANDY SCHNEI
BEGINNER TO ADVANCED
Because knowledge is Forever.
SeeingMusicBooks.com
SEEING MUSIC
METHOD BOOKS

Chord and Note Reference

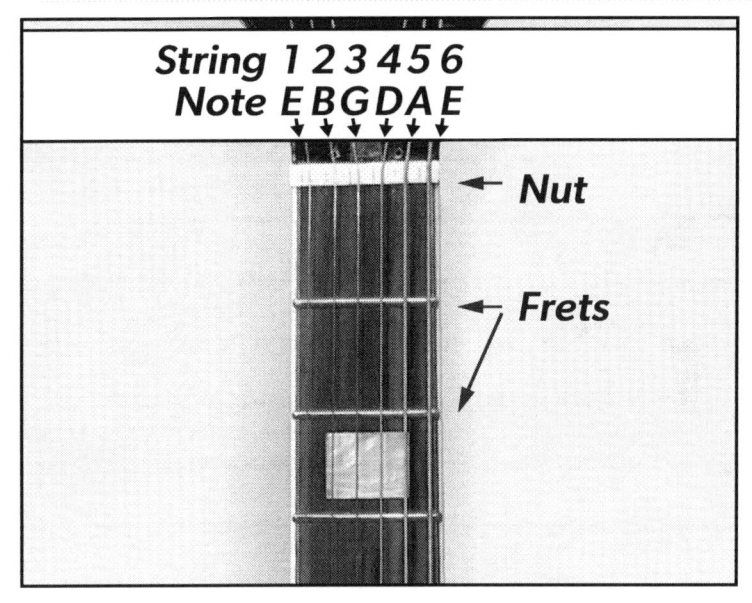

Fig.172 - Standard Guitar Tuning

String 1 2 3 4 5 6
Note E B G D A E

Nut

Frets

Common Guitar Tunings - low to high

Standard	E A D G B E
E-flat Standard	E♭ A♭ D♭ G♭ B♭ E♭
DADGAD	D A D G A D
Drop D	D A D G B E
Open G	D G D G B D

Fig.173 - Common Guitar Tunings

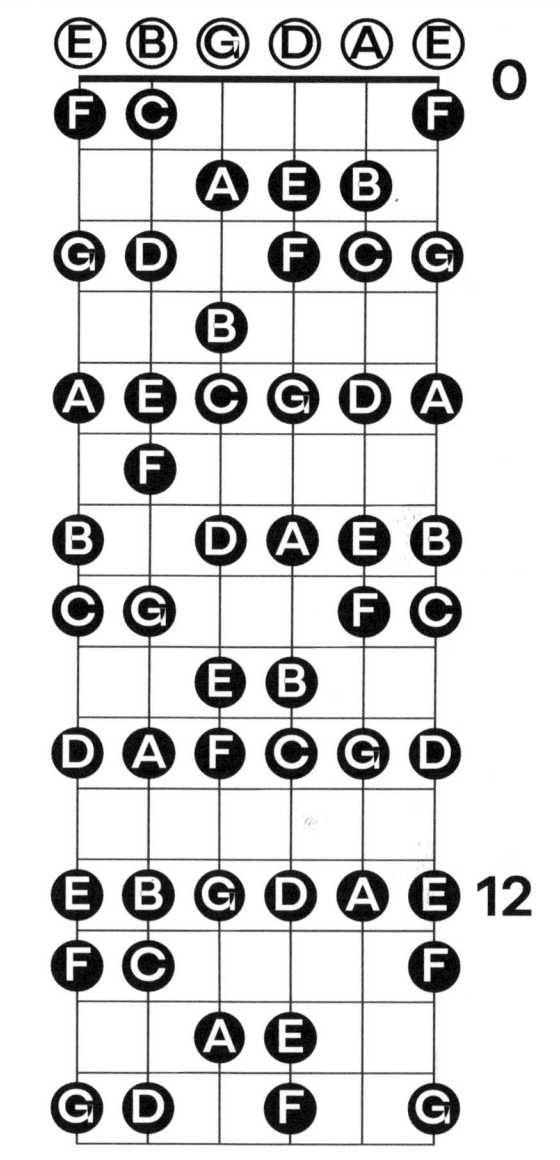

Fig.175 - Natural Notes of the Guitar

Fig.174 - Chord Diagram Elements

Nut (Thick line)
Frets (Horizontal Lines)
Strings (Vertical Lines)
O's - Play Open-string
X's - String is not used, don't play
Black Dots - Place fingers here

CHORD AND NOTE REFERENCE 75

Open-String or Barre   Easy

A Major

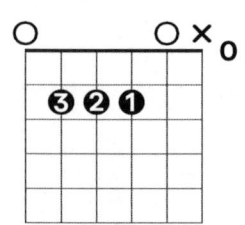

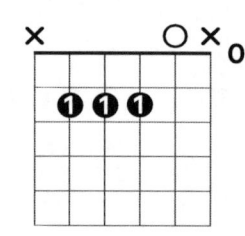

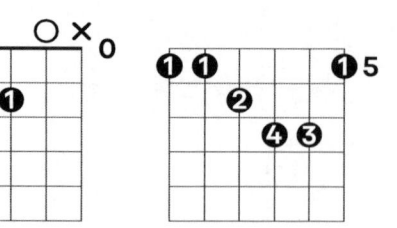

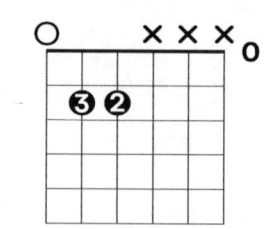

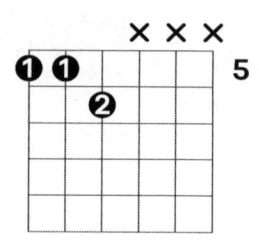

A Minor

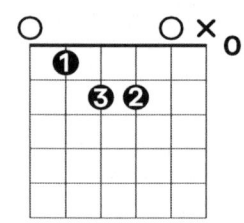

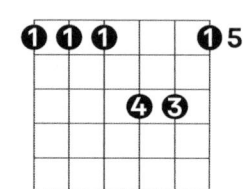

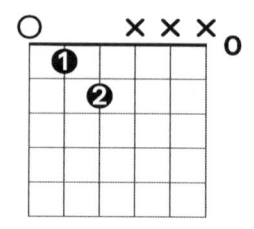

A7

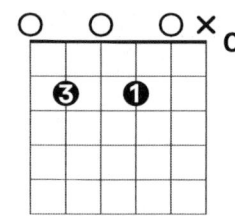

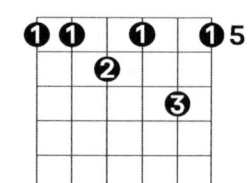

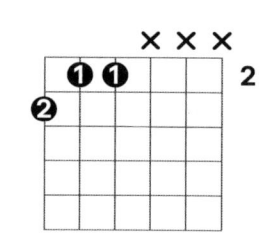

B-flat Major

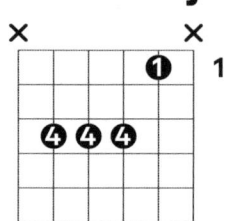

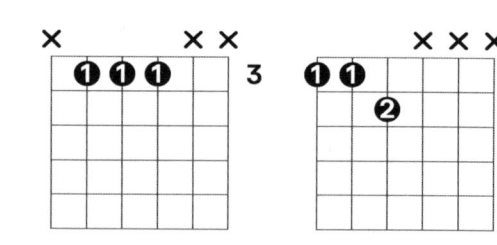

B Major

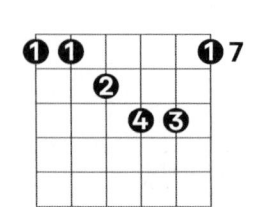

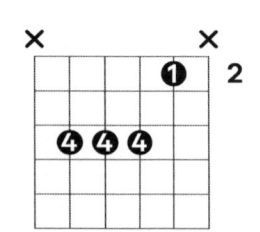

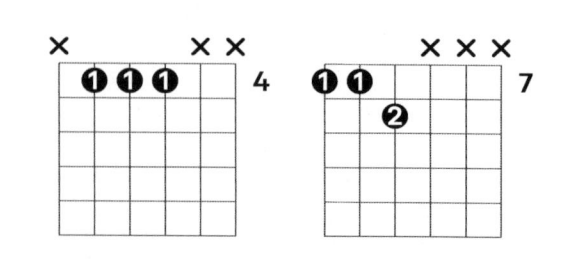

76 Electric Guitar for Left-Handed Adults - Book 1 - Seeing Music Method Books

Open-String or Barre   *Easy*

B Minor

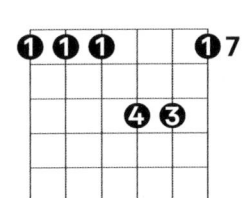

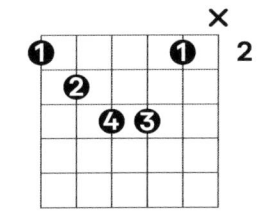

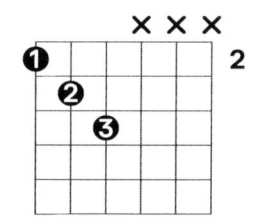

C Major

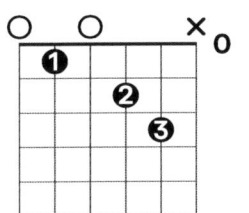

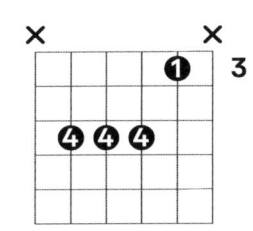

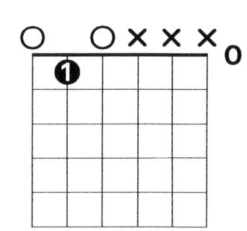

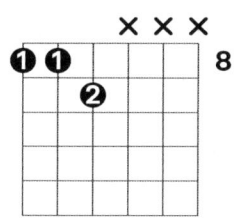

C Minor

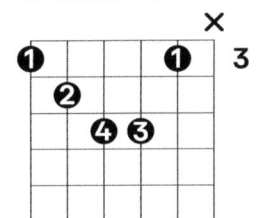

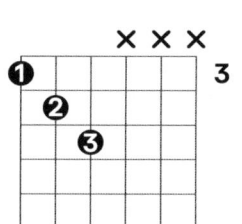

C⁷

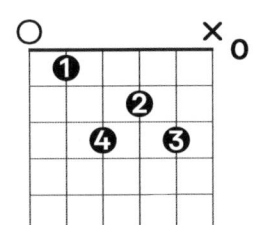

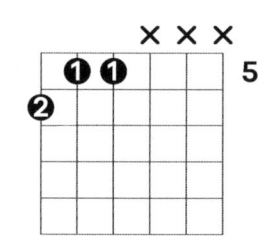

C^Maj7

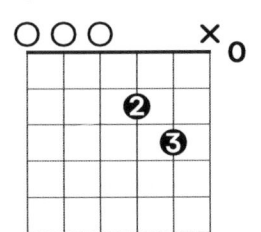

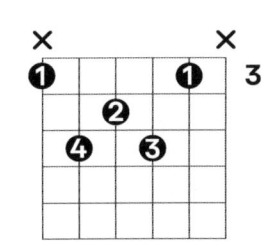

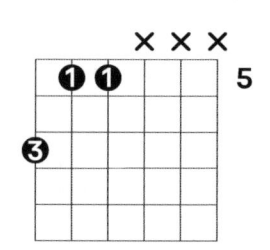

CHORD AND NOTE REFERENCE 77

Open-String or Barre *Easy*

D Major

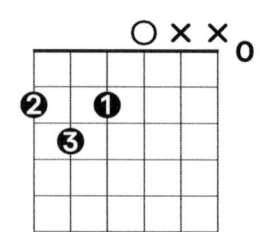

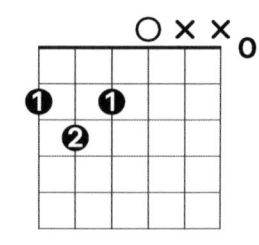

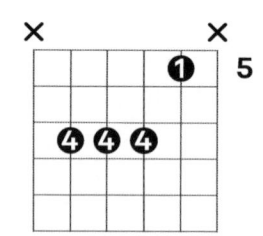

D Minor

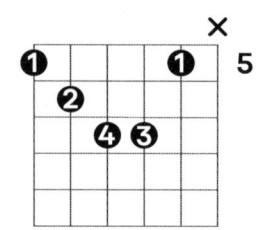

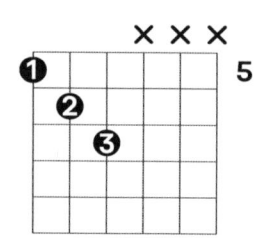

D7

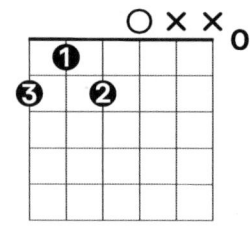

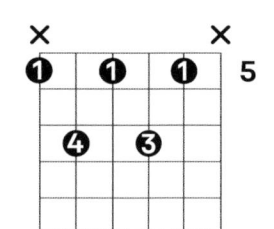

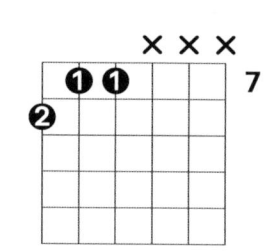

E Major

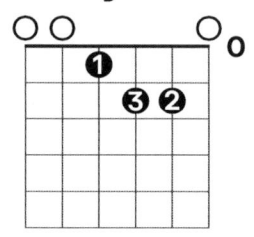

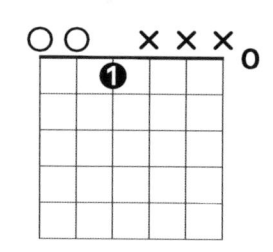

E Minor

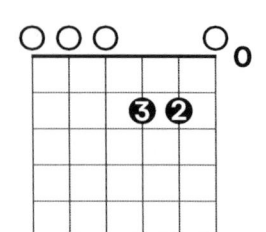

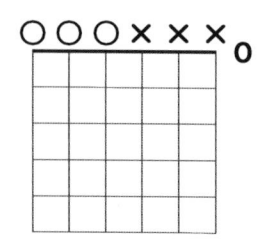

78 Electric Guitar for Left-Handed Adults - Book 1 - Seeing Music Method Books

Open-String or Barre **Easy**

F Major

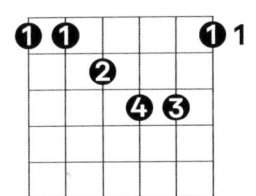

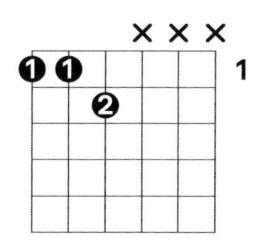

G Major

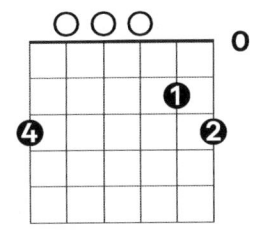

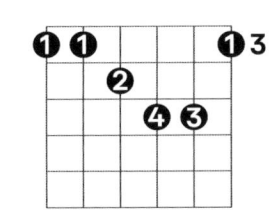

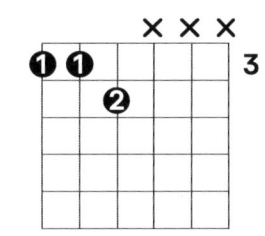

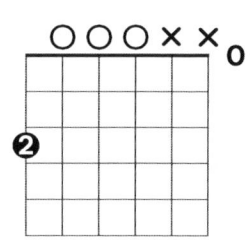

G Minor

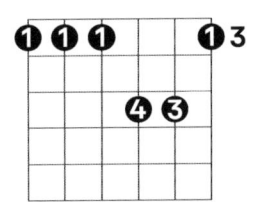

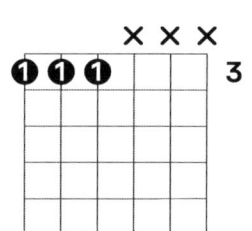

G7

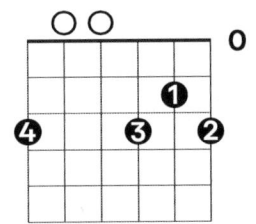

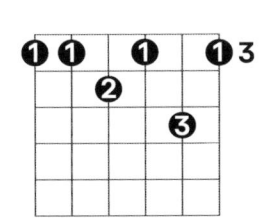

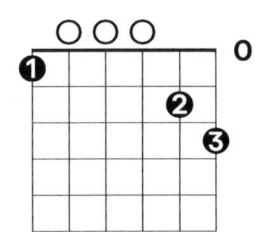

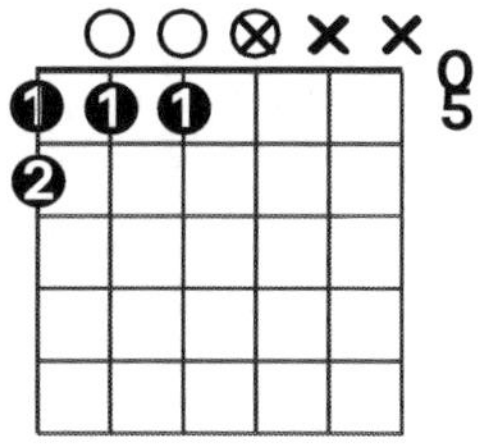

CHORD AND NOTE REFERENCE 79

Thanks and congratulations on your purchase of this book! Here are your streaming lesson videos.

Visit: https://seeingmusicbooks.com/r9v5w1h6p

1 For access to the lesson videos, scan this QR or visit the URL above

2 Register for our website, FREE at seeingmusicbooks.com

3 Watch the lesson videos on any computer or device logged-in to seeingmusicbooks.com

80 ELECTRIC GUITAR FOR LEFT-HANDED ADULTS - BOOK 1 - SEEING MUSIC METHOD BOOKS

Printed in Great Britain
by Amazon